LAUGHING IN STITCHES

ED KAISER

ISBN 978-0-9891462-9-6
Printed in the USA

Published by Buttonwood Press, LLC
P.O. Box 716, Haslett, Michigan 48840
www.buttonwoodpress.com

ACKNOWLEDGEMENTS:

Is there any connection between a semi-colon and the large intestine?

Heading the list of those to whom I am indebted for their part in this book must be the doctors, nurses, radiologists, specialists, technicians, EMTs, NPs, MAs and PAs...even my own familial Ma and Pa. For without all of them — and a few health care providers for whom I don't recall their titles — I would not be here today. Nor would I have humorous stories to share about them.

There is one non-medical doctor who I am deeply indebted to. Dr. Richard L Baldwin saved me from the plague of unpublished authors... obscurus incognitis. Under his care, encouragement and unwavering support of me and his directorship of Buttonwood Press, I no longer suffer from obscurity.

Another doctor I am grateful to William D. Strempel, Dean of Michigan State University's College of Osteopathic Medicine and Mary Kay Smith, Director, MSU Learning and Assessment Center. Without their expressed consent, I could not have shared the anecdotes involving doctors and nurses in training.

The text that my fingers transcribe from my mind's dictation is systemically infected and cannot be left untreated. I must acknowledge those who skillfully treated my chronic writing maladies. Wendie

Karpinski is my grammarian—you know…Their the won whom our bettor then a spell-checker. Effectively, Wendie provided cosmetic surgery to all the ugly blemishes my stories were born with. Ooops, I mean, with which my manuscript was borne.

Though Wendie's prescriptions quelled the infections, there was still a fear of debilitating comas…no, that's commas. So a proofreader was added to the trauma team. Joyce Wagner surgically removed tainted text and transplanted punctuations with meticulous precision. There was a lot of bloodletting in this procedure. Well…at least there was plenty of red on the *sheets*.

Once the body of my text was saved from the morgue, typesetter Marie Kar set all fractured paragraphs into functional alignment and transferred the embodiment of my humorous accounts to Color House Graphics, Grand Rapids, MI for binding and outpatient services.

Even if my writing afflictions are not cured, I am most certainly appreciative of this team's therapeutic massages.

I dedicate this book to all the medical practitioners who have never failed to provide me excellent care as well as favorable conditions for humor. This book is my opportunity to give them a shot.

PREFACE

It is not the jokes we tell, it is sharing humorous life experiences which endears us to each other.

Laughing in Stitches is almost entirely about my physical well being...or lack thereof. Rather than clutter frivolous stories with intellectual medical digests, I shall divulge some rather key information here in this preface.

I have a genetic mutation. If you count my brains being in the shallow end of the gene pool, then I have two mutations. Even if my mental reality check bounces, the more serious gene defect is the propensity for my blood to clot. However illogical it may seem, to forestall potentially fatal clotting, I am on a steady diet of rat poison... medicinally known as Warfarin — a blood thinner.

In addition to being susceptible to blood clots, I have another chronic disorder. Apnea. My supposition is that Apnea occurs when the breathing function of the autonomic system becomes autocratic. Though no journal of medicine has investigated my supposition, I wonder if the diaphragm feels like it is not fully appreciated by the lungs, so it goes on strike. Maybe it's the unionized worker cells of the diaphragm against the frequently inflated ego of managerial lungs.

Whatever anatomical function failure might be the cause, the effect is a cessation of inhale.

At least no air is drawn into the lungs until the brain—Chief Executive Officer—senses oxygen deprivation and sends a scathing message ordering a return to work. The diaphragm reacts with a sudden and forceful withdrawal in the opposite direction of the lungs... commonly recognized as a gasp. This resumption of cyclic inhale and exhale negates a potentially terminal condition. Coincidentally, it also terminates my wife's phone investigation of my Life Insurance coverage.

All of the stories in this book are true. However far-fetched they may seem, each occurred shortly before my writing of the account. They were originally authored as a weekly issue of "Friday Frivolity"— an e-mailed bit of humor I have distributed for over 15 years. Thus, some of the stories begin as if the reader has read other missives from me. I have also attempted to order the stories in this book chronologically from 15 years ago to date.

There are a few exceptions to the whole truth of the narratives. Specifically, this exclusion is in regard to stories involving my portrayals as a Standardized Patient. I am privileged to serve my Alma Mater, Michigan State University, by simulating certain maladies for its Colleges of Nursing, Human, Osteopathic and Veterinarian Medicine. Okay, so maybe I don't actually simulate any canine or feline afflictions, but I have portrayed the owner of some.

Therefore, the half-truth of these special stories is that the interactions are authentic, while the malady is fictional. These "simulated cases" are specifically portrayed to assist the student's edification. Briefly, as a Standardized Patient, SP, I am trained to depict a particular scenario for future health care providers to practice communication and examination skills.

In effect, this provides a safe and supportive environment for learners. Student privacy is strictly guarded. Therefore, I use extreme caution with the text of the four SP stories included herein.

Also, these particular narratives are generally compilations. That is, no story involves, or even remotely identifies, a single student. Rather they are accumulated instances of humor from roles I have portrayed over the past eight years at five different campuses. Effectively then, these tales are fictional, per se.

I include these stories with the permission of Michigan State University and solely for the humor content. In no way should these chronicles adversely reflect on the University's Medical Colleges, its faculty, the Learning and Assessment Center personnel, or students endeavoring to become proficient Medical Practitioners.

Each story is preceded by a **? of the day**. These are typically rhetorical. Some of these mind-bending questions you may have heard before. Some are conjured up in the ebb and flow of brain waves in my mental ocean, causing a severe undertow. I hope none of them drag you under. I'd much rather you find a warm spot on a sandy beach, lie comfortably on a blanket, and use the book to shade your eyes than to strain your mind wondering **If someone waves a fee, is the surf up?**

QUESTION OF THE DAY:

If you go to an optometrist but can't read the sign, how do you know if you're in the right place?

But this question is practically irrelevant. For if my vision is so poor that I cannot read the sign, my wife should be leading me by the hand and she would be deciding which door to enter. It was good that Sue accompanied me on a recent visit to the optometrist. I clearly read the sign: **Walk-Ins Welcome ~ The Optometrist Is In**. After that, everything else became blurred in my-oh-my myopic mind.

1

Oh... Now I see

It had reached a point that regardless of how clean the lenses of my glasses were, many things in my view seemed a bit smudged. Especially in my right eye. Why one eye would deteriorate more quickly than the other was a matter for the optometrist to explain.

Whether he could actually explain it or not, I was quite certain I needed new glasses. Although the prospects of needing new glasses is not fearful, I am never particularly excited about the testing. There's something about accurately reading the tiniest print on the chart that I associate with machismo. So, after the optometrist had set the dual lenses of his analytic monstrosity to my current lens prescriptions, he positioned my chin, aligned the peep-holes to my eyeball-spacing and asked, "What is the smallest line you can read?"

"E."

That's the truth. Every line beneath that single letter at the pinnacle of the chart progressively diminished from fuzzy to a miniscule Wingding font. Even two lines down I couldn't tell the difference between 8, B, or even E. In a sentence, context tells me if it's a 2 or a Z. But there were no sentences on the chart…I thought they were names in a foreign language.

Then he started flipping the lenses on one eye while obscuring the other eye's vision. He patiently went back and forth with "Number 1… or Number 2?" To me, the variance was so subtle my right eye went to sleep while my left eye deliberated between what's behind door Number One…or does Door Two have a bigger prize.

Finally he finished evaluating both eyes and advised me he wanted to check for cataracts. I agreed. He said he needed to put some drops in my eyes first. As the initial drop onto my right eye ignited a fire on my eyeball, he predicted, "This may sting a little."

Immediately, my left eye clamped shut as tight as a startled clam. Somehow, he managed to wedge open both eyes for a few drops of dilating fluid in each. It would take several minutes for my pupils to dilate sufficiently for his clear inspection of my cataracts. He suggested I go out to the waiting room to investigate frames for my new glasses.

There certainly were plenty to choose from. I selected a prospective frame and replaced my current glasses with them. Did I mention that the top line, single letter, "E" was all I could clearly attest to WITH my glasses on? I don't need to mention that the prospective frames had clear lenses.

I was not sure if it was me in a mirror or a picture of some really cool guy modeling a particular brand of glasses. Okay, so maybe I did get a bit of a glare-back that identified it was indeed my bald pate in a mirror. However, the frames were only noticeable from the pressure on my nose, not the image in the mirror. The solution was to let Sue decide. That made sense anyway as she has the best judgment as to how any given frame affects my appearance.

Soon, my eyes were dilated enough for me to find my way out of Carlsbad Caverns during a power failure. I easily negotiated back to the chair in his graciously dimly-lit lab. After the optometrist finished the cataract exam—which apparently required him to use a light beam capable of reflecting off of my retina far into outer space.

Back to the waiting room. My eyes alternated from blurring tears to seeing flickering light beams of return messages from deep space aliens.

Paying the bill was the last thing to do before Sue could drive me home. She did not need to have her eyes dilated. However, she did have her eyesight evaluated and was also purchasing new glasses...and sun glasses as well. With my old glasses in place, I reviewed the bill.

I did not recall the optometrist mentioning double vision, but the billing certainly indicated I was now afflicted with that malady also. Nearly every line on the bill which detailed Sue's purchases and mine was duplicated. When I inquired as to why that was the case, the sales representative stated that each lens is priced separately.

Wait just a cotton-pickin' minute. I may not be able to see clearly, but my mind's eye doesn't need corrective lenses yet. "Are you telling me that I'm not buying a pair of lenses?" I skeptically asked. "I'm buying them one by one?" "Wow," I mentioned to Sue. "Let's just get me a lens for my right eye. It's the worst of the two. I'll wait for next month's paycheck to come back for the left lens."

I wondered if they would provide me a patch to wear in the meantime. I'll pretend to be a pirate who scratched an itchy eye with his hook.

Actually I should have asked for two patches. I thought the store lighting was bright until I went outside. Next time, I'm scheduling a night appointment.

QUESTION OF THE DAY:

How did I manage to get over the hill without ever getting to the top?

I do not wish to complain, but in getting over the hill I have traipsed through quite a few medical fields. I've had a couple off-the-trail treks to ER. Nevertheless, I have tried to find humor in the weeds on the hillside. I do not intend to downplay anyone's physical infirmity, yet I often try to apply a little salve of humor to lessen the emotional stress their illness may cause them. Such was the case when a friend wrote me of her frustration with a medical woe that doctors were not having much luck alleviating. Because, at that time, I also was experiencing symptoms that perplexed my doctor, I wrote the following to her.

2

Medical Woes

I believe we are stumping our respective physicians as they endeavor to discover what is causing our un-respective ailments. They may not know the cause, but seem to believe we can help their diagnoses by giving something up.

So what to give up? Hmmm, when I was a young man, I drank way too much Detroit River Water, smoked everything from vines to stogies, and consumed enough cholesterol to clog the Windsor Tunnel. Not to mention my frequent habit of carousing around 'til all hours of the night chasing all manner of women… and a few without manners!

And, that was just my college years.

In my twenties and thirties, I added overindulgence of sugar and salt as well as escalating most of my other bad habits to just short of excessive. At least, in my estimation, it was less than excessive. I cannot exactly recall libation to the extent of being drunk. Of course, there were times when I could not recall falling down, either.

Such a wild and glorious lifestyle has its price. Ironically, it also provides remedy. Through the years, as one affliction after another would wage war on my well-being, I would simply give up one of my vices and feel better for it.

My misfortune, at the moment, is that I have no vice in reserve to offer as sacrifice for my current ailment. No whiskey left to water the flowers at Dionysus' shrine. No cigars remain in my humidor to burn on the altar of Apollo—not that Apollo even closely resembles a physique I could possibly hope for; nonetheless he is the Greek god of health.

Inasmuch as I currently have nothing to sacrifice to appease the ire of Apollo, I am at an impasse. Perhaps I should have clung to a few evil habits so the doctor could find something for me to renounce.

The last time I went to the doctor, Sue told him I would stop breathing as I slept. Oh… my… goodness! I thought he was going to have a medical rapture. He scrambled for a pen to take note of a repeatable symptom he could analyze. He was almost jubilant with the prospect of something specific to treat.

He asked her how long the cessation of breathing would last.

"Well," Sue said, "He usually struggles for a minute or so, but finally manages to get my hands off his throat."

So much for his thoughts of apnea being the cause of my medical woe.

QUESTION OF THE DAY:

If you're feeling blue, shouldn't you consider taking a deep breath?

Though Apnea happens during sleep, I can only suppose that blue is applicable to my appearance as well as my emotional state.

Did you read the Preface? I know, many readers do not. Often a Preface is strewn with a lengthy explanation of the author's rationale for the book. Rational thinking is not applicable to most of what I write, so I used the opening paragraphs of this book to explain some of the issues about my health—like Apnea.

If you don't read the Preface, you may not fully understand my relationship with such things as CPAP. But then, even reading my Preface, does not ensure your enlightenment with regard to medical terminology. However, it will give you a clearer understanding of what ails me physically …if not mentally.

3

Sleep Study

I had a "sleep deprivation study" done. It was accomplished in two phases. On my first visit, they wired me up to check temperature, blood oxygen, respiration rate & volume, eye movement, EKG, EEG, …GEE, I think they could have even told me when my bladder was full!

Not that I needed that particular piece of information, but they would if my bladder bloated during the night. The overnight monitoring nurse would need plenty of advanced warning to get all the wires unhooked, STAT, should I feel the urge.

Anyway, I had a hundred wires glued at 3-inch intervals from the top of my head to my heels and the nurse told me to relax and go to sleep. Riiiight! Maybe somebody who's into bondage would have drifted right off into dreamland, but not me.

As I lay there trying to count sheep, I kept thinking about the woman at the other end of all my wires, watching a computer screen that's reporting even the slightest twitch of my eyeballs. My perverted sense of humor wondered what the monitor might look like if I conjured up some X-rated fantasy.

Eventually I became accustomed to the spaghetti draped over my meatball skull, and fell asleep. Even though I don't recall experiencing… or conjuring up, any euphoric dreams, I did spend a fairly restful night.

At least it was about as restful as I would normally get at home. Unfortunately, the computer reported that I did have occurrences of apnea. None were severe, but significant enough to warrant the second test.

The second visit was almost identical to the first, except this time they also hooked up a hose to inflate me. Actually, the hose was the exhaust of a CPAP machine.

It must have improved my sleep study results because the doctor prescribed my very own Continuous Positive Airway Pressure: CPAP.

Every night, I put on a nose mask that resembles a diver's SCUBA. It's good that I don't have to wear goggles lest Sue be tempted to douse me with water when I fail to keep my mouth closed. Aside from Sue's temptation, anatomically, if I fail to keep my mouth closed, it enables a pressurized wind tunnel from the CPAP machine, through the hose connected to my face mask, past my uvula and exhausts through my open mouth — otherwise known as an obnoxious snore.

If I do keep my mouth shut, the CPAP is supposed to give me a comfortable, restful, full night of sleep. I'm not sure exactly how that happens. I don't know… maybe it's supposed to inflate me enough to… like… hover over the mattress. Makes me wonder if a CPAP ad might be:

Ladies and gentlemen! Do you toss and turn all night? Do you wake up tired and listless? Are you tired of bobbing like driftwood on your water bed?.

Then enter the new millennium! Operators are standing by to take your order for CPAP... the one and only AIR BED.

Hover blissfully through the night and wake up rested, rejuvenated, and ready to hit the ground running. (Of course, if you shut the machine off before you start running, you'll hit the ground with a resounding thud.)

Your CPAP has enough pressure to open clogged nasal passages. It'll literally knock the snot out of you.

And, as an added bonus... if you order right now, we'll include, at no extra charge, our handy-dandy, 3-foot tether. It will keep you in the bedroom in case your wife leaves the window open.

So, don't wake up stiff, sore, and irritable ever again. Hover in tranquility through the night with CPAP !

Hovering or not, I can't quite figure out how anybody could get comfortable with a hose clamped over his nose. Maybe I missed something in the instruction book. Do you think I should have the hose hooked up to a helium bottle rather than ambient air? Hey, a little laughing gas would seem quite appropriate, wouldn't it?

QUESTION OF THE DAY:

Did Dr. Jekyll ever really feel like himself?

There really are no Jekyll & Hyde nurses. At least I've not encountered any with split personalities. That is not to say that some hospital personnel may impose dual standards.

4

Dual Standards

I'm back home now and will immediately initiate a full investigation of a certain hospital's policies. I am appalled at the dual standard which I discovered during my overnight stay. There is a conspiracy against men and I fully intend to expose it.

Here's a true account of what happened. At least I'll report the pertinent details. I needed nasal surgery. My sinus cavities needed more drainage holes. For some, such a minor procedure would be outpatient surgery. However, because I suffer from apnea, my surgeon wanted me to spend the night, just to be safe. Considering he had thrashed about my sinus cavities for nearly two hours, combined with my susceptibility to involuntary cessation of breathing, he thought it would be wise to have me monitored while I slept—necessarily without my CPAP.

After regaining my senses following surgery, one of the recovery nurses transported me to a room for an overnight stay.

By the time she wheeled me into the room, I was ready for food. Any food. I had not eaten in the last 24 hours and was eager to do so. What a delight to find a 5-page, leather-bound, menu on my bed tray.

I quickly leafed through the pages, mentioning to Sue some of the delectable entrées I spotted. My joy was short-lived as the nurse snatched it from my grasp. "That's not your menu, Ed. It is only for women."

"Whoa… hold on. Just for women?" I retorted.

"Yes. This is the maternity unit and I don't believe you are pregnant."

What a relief that bit of news was to me. Anesthesia does sometimes give a person a false sense of reality. So it was a relief to know that the surgeon had not implanted an alien in my abdomen while I was out.

However, the nurse's revelation did not seem particularly relevant to the menu I was drooling over. So, I inquired, "What's that got to do with eating? I need nourishment to facilitate my recovery and the steak dinner I saw in there should do quite nicely, thank you."

"I'll bring you some Jell-O," she stated emphatically.

"Jell-O? I don't want Jell-O. I want steak!"

She bluntly reiterated, "I told you, women order from that menu."

"Come'ere, Sue," I said to my wife. "I'll sit in the birthing chair; you jump in bed and order."

I guess you know I got Jell-O.

After an hour of earnest pleading, Clara Barton replaced Kathy Bates to relieve my misery. The night nurse was far more compassionate and relented to bring me supper.

Oh, sure…Supper. Really? Popsicle, broth and juice. I had surgery on my nose, not my esophagus. "I need sustenance not sauce."

Incidentally, my doctor had put a wad of gauze below my nose. Ever try a liquid diet with cloth draped from your upper lip? I think the gauze got more of the popsicle than I did. Cherry Jell-O and strawberry popsicle may indeed be a delightful blend of flavoring. However, red-stained gauze dripping from my nostrils would not be particularly appealing to visitors—of which there were none. Spouses only allowed in the maternity wing.

It's a conspiracy, I tell you! Women the world over will deny it. Most still profess it's a man's world. Well, I will testify to the *Grandiose Jury* that it is most certainly not a man's world in the maternity wing. I felt exiled. A male held captive in a tower ruled by women. Despite plush chairs for expectant mothers, I was relegated to a steel-railed bed.

QUESTION OF THE DAY:

Why is it when someone tastes something awful, they want you to taste it too?

Taste is a much higher priority when someone else is fixing a meal than when I fix something for myself. My culinary protocol is open, heat and eat. No pinch of salt. No dash of pepper. If it's not in the can, it's not for lunch. My wife Sue, however, can taste the difference between a pinch and dash.

5

Soup for Lunch

Once, shortly after we were married, Sue was ill. Earnestly desiring to impress her with my care giving, I wandered into the kitchen to fix her lunch.

I say "wandered" as the kitchen is a strange land for me to visit without a guide. In my basement workroom, I can locate hand tools with my eyes shut, find the appropriate fastener with the proficiency of a voice-activated robot, and know where every power tool is stored. That is my homeland.

The kitchen is across the border. Regardless that the instructional words on cans, boxes and documents in the kitchen appear to be in English, I am unable to properly translate the subtle variances of stir, mix, blend and fold. Oh, but I've got "beat" quite clear in my mind. Yeaaah…the difference between beat and whoop are visually acute in my masculine mind. However, to my mind, the kitchen instruction to "beat" is in an ambiguous category with whip, puree and whisk. (Though at one time, I thought whisking was what my mom did to me, with a broom, when she wanted me out of her kitchen.)

Considering that Sue—border guard, guide and translator, was languishing in bed, I needed to fix something I was familiar with. Soup and fruit seemed like a good choice. Fruit was quite easy. Get out the trusty "never-needs-sharpening-slice-everything-effortlessly" knife and whack away. Wow, it really looked easy on TV.

After I put on a band-aid and tossed out the red-blotched banana pieces, I took a much slower approach to the apple. Even if not picture-perfect slicing and dicing, fruit-cutting was completed without further mishap.

Soup is not particularly challenging to me. The Campbell kids often join me for lunch. They are advocates of my open, heat, and eat protocol.

I was one proud guy to escape the kitchen without a fire or bloody stub—the cut should heal sooner than the burn. Do you know how fast water boils in a dish rag mopping up a little spill on a glass-top burner?

My task of fixing lunch for my ailing wife was complete. I even made a delectable-looking arrangement on the tray with the fruit, crackers, and some cheese. Then, with the decorum of Jeeves, and a chest rivaling a ruffed grouse, I strutted into the bedroom with her lunch.

She was so grateful.

Initially, anyway.

Upon sampling the tomato soup she inquired as to what I had used to dilute it.

I proudly responded, "Dilute it? Oh, no, dear, I didn't water it down."

"Then how much milk did you use?"

"Ahhhh, milk? I didn't use milk, either. I didn't want to weaken the soup, hon. You need all the nutrients you can get from each spoonful."

She quickly rose up in bed. I was quite amazed that only one spoonful of soup would result in such expedience in her recovery.

"What part of concentrate don't you understand?"

"Concentrate? On what?" I meekly offered as the air noticeably hissed from my deflating chest.

"Concentrate on what it says on the label. Dilute with one can of milk."

Well, that was it. No more kitchen privileges for me. At least not unsupervised.

Sue's in control of the kitchen. I cook outside. Fewer dials, settings, and no recipes to follow. Toss it on, keep the flash fires under control, and pull it off while the meat's still limber enough to chew. That's about all the cookin' I can be trusted with.

QUESTION OF THE DAY:

After you get out of sorts, do you remember going in?

Generally speaking, whenever I am out of sorts and about to seek medical attention, I'll get encouraging e-mail. Here is my response to one such instance of encouragement, during my hospital stay, while recovering from pulmonary emboli.

6

Patient Patient

Okay, you've said all the right things. Be careful. Mind the doctors. Listen to Sue. But you failed to mention "be patient."

It's a good thing you overlooked that trite admonition. After being warned of the risk of fatality if I left the bed, being careful was a given. Also, concerning this prohibition of movement, it was not a burly nurse who threatened my life. Rather, it was the blood clots in my lungs which put me in jeopardy.

Continuing in regard to your counsel, I am always very attentive to the advice of doctors and I always listen to Sue. Although, admittedly, my hearing aids do not always function properly regarding Sue's voice. That is especially true when thundering waterfalls inspire great photo opportunities from mid-river rocks, as well as drowning out her voice—especially her enunciation of "DON'T."

In the matter of being a patient patient, that's rather oxymoronic where I am concerned. I have a hard time waiting for super glue to set up. Well…usually, anyway. I reluctantly confess that I once simultaneously adhered my thumb and forefinger to the joint-line while repairing a decapitated miniature figurine. Despite this regrettable exception to my impatience with glue drying, allowing time to elapse in medical matters isn't any easier.

When the ER doctor said 7-10 days in bed, I began to hyperventilate and quickly voiced my disapproval. At that moment, I didn't realize the dangers of lung clots and the necessity of remaining sessile. When he emphatically stated "Pulmonary embolism can be fatal," I got a whole new perspective, laid back on the gurney, and waited for the drugs to take hold.

Days 1 and 2 were in the record books before I really knew they had occurred. Whilst I was on drugs for the pain, I hardly felt the bed under me so that doesn't really count as being in bed. Besides, if you don't know what day it is, it's hard to count them.

However, when the stupor wore off, I became quite restless. Patience evaporated along with the fog previously hanging low in my brain. In my mind, no pain meant the danger due to the clots had also vaporized. I could clearly see the path to the bathroom. I ought to be able to walk that far at least.

Yeah, sure, I remembered the original prognosis that I'd likely be in bed 7 to 10 days. Yet now, with the drug-induced fog lifting, I could see a brighter dawn of Day 3. I felt I was recuperating quicker than projected. I began to lobby for a more reasonable sentencing of 5-7.

With my legs twitching in spasmodic protest and my soles crying out for the opportunity just to feel the cold floor, I beseeched the nurse for a 2-minute stand. I might have had better luck calling Dial-a-Prayer. "Please be patient, Mr. Kaiser. We need to get your Coumadin dosage leveled."

"What's my getting out of bed got to do with the level of rat poison in my system?" I protested. "Will all the Coumadin sink into my legs if I stand up?"

"No, but we must get a balance of your medications and a steady pro-thrombin time before you can get out of bed."

"Balance my meds? *Prothrobin*? I promise my feet won't be throbbin' if I get up and you can put three pill bottles in each hand for the balance test," I pleaded.

She smiled, but her chuckle closely resembled the sound of a judge's gavel signaling the end of my plea bargain.

Finally, late in Day 4, they relented to allow me a trip to the bathroom. I was overjoyed at the prospect. That is, until I closed the bathroom door. I am not a seasoned hospital veteran. I have had zero experiential learning of how to effectively prepare for the task at hand. You see, this bout with blood clots occurred shortly after my shoulder surgery.

I effectively had just one hand as my left arm was still in a sling. Try to picture a one-armed guy with a heart monitor sagging his hospital gown to obstruct necessary vision of everything below his chin. Add to that a wire harness, IV, and catheter while trying to intermittently grasp the IV stand and tug on his shorts without plunging headlong into the door…or abruptly seating himself prematurely.

I believe that experience fostered a much higher degree of patience for me. I became much more tolerant of the necessary elapse of time to safely aid my recovery. Becoming a patient patient rewarded me with an early release at Day 5.

QUESTION OF THE DAY:

Does it hurt to kick the bucket if you die with your boots on?

I normally have a positive outlook. The inevitability of my kicking the bucket is less likely to torment me than trying to resolve this **? of the day**. However, there were occasions during my first bout with blood clots that did cause me to wonder if I should put my boots on.

7

Change of Venue

Continuing the saga of my encounter with PE—that is, Pulmonary Emboli, otherwise known as blood clots in the lungs,

Frequent visits by nurses inquiring, "Are you in pain,...having trouble breathing,...is there anything I can do for you?" seemed to always be accompanied by concerned expressions. It was a bit scary for a while.

After several days of very attentive care, a nurse came into my room to announce that things were about to change for me. Not that I was unhappy with my previous room service, but I considered change as a good omen. Maybe even that I could finally get out of bed.

My spirits rose quickly. She turned to squarely face me. I was hopeful she would inquire: "Would you like to get up?"

I was not so lucky. She matter-of-factly announced, "You're going to have a change of venue. We're going to move you out of this room." I don't know whether her cappuccino got cold or someone stepped on her last nerve, but she was not particularly encouraging with her proclamation.

She disappeared before I could ask for clarification. My luck hadn't just slumped, it had collapsed in a heap on the floor. My pulse went down almost as quickly as my luck. The BP-cuff on my arm registered 90 over nothin'. Could my condition possibly deteriorate further?

My new room was at the opposite end of 6-North. As they wheeled my bed into the room, I couldn't help but notice the furniture…or the absence thereof. No chairs for visitors? Could it be that I was being quarantined? Considering how often I had harassed my nurses during the week, I probably deserved detention…but isolation?

Because I was still on restriction—no ambulation without supervision, I asked the orderly who was locking my bed into position if he would accompany me to the bathroom.

"You can't use this bathroom," came his succinct reply.

"Why not?" I logically countered.

"It's full of furniture."

"Furniture? You don't think I'm going to entertain visitors in there, do you?" I illogically retorted.

As he left the room he offered, "I'll go ask the nurse."

What? It takes an RN to decide where my visitors are to sit? I may have a physical malady, but my senses are intact. I've been known to meditate in the bathroom, but conversations are limited to telepathic internal messages or occasional vocalized utterances that are better understood in pig pens. What sense is bathroom seating for more than one person. Let's face it, when was the last time you greeted a visitor to your home with, "Hi! It's nice that you could stop by. Let's go in the bathroom and chat a while before dinner."

So there I sat in a barren room. No end table. They hadn't even wheeled in my bed tray yet. Hey, that's where my crossword book sat. Even if my time is short, I need the mental diversion of crossword puzzles. I pushed the call button on the remote.

Oh, and speaking of the remote, it would not turn on the TV. Consequently, I wondered if it registered my call at the nurses' station. I checked the buttons on the remote for control of the lights. No luck. *I'm in solitary. I wonder if Sue knows the dire condition of my health. I thought back to when the orderly walked away from my room. Was the diminishing echo of his footsteps a harbinger of my future? Was my well-being also fading into the distance?*

It surely was a distance to the nurse's station and one not often traversed. No nurses or aides strolled in to ask of my condition or needs. In fact, nobody would even respond to the call button. My remote was a functionless piece of plastic.

I was now secluded in the far reaches of 6-North. Voices were faint and far down the corridor. No traffic in the hall outside my door. I believed that I had turned a corner. Turned a corner, but what road was I going down?

Either I was no longer in a life-threatening condition or my pastor would be in shortly with last rites.

My mental jury was still deliberating when the judge entered my room. The judge…in the personage of my pastor, seemed to be the swaying vote. Not only was he my first visitor following my change of venue, he was carrying his portable Communion kit. If he had been wearing a white robe, I would have succumbed immediately.

Turns out that my change of venue was to make room for a patient requiring more care than I needed. I was out of jeopardy and watchful care was no longer necessary.

QUESTION OF THE DAY:

How did a fool and his money get together in the first place?

American capitalism is based upon money. Hippocratic oath aside, doctors must give consideration to the monetary aspects of their business as much as they do to focusing on diagnoses of physical symptoms. As is often the case with me, my symptoms don't make any more sense to them than their "rules" do to me.

8

Semantics

Went to the doctor yesterday. No big deal. Sore throat that I didn't want to get worse. When we arrived, the office was on a lunch break so I whiled away some time reading posted notices on the glass at the receptionist's desk.

One in particular intrigued me. Item 1 read, **You must pay your co-pay <u>before</u> seeing the doctor.** Now I'm not sure how long the notice had been up there. Without a doubt, it had been quite some time. I had just not bothered to read it before.

Not only had I never read it, I had never paid my co-pay before seeing the doctor. Though it had not previously crossed my mind, holding off on full payment is a sound business practice. But then, dealing with a doctor is hardly like hiring a plumber. If the drip continues after the plumber's done, full payment is undeserved. However, effective stoppage of post nasal drip takes more time than a single office visit.

So, though I've not paid doctors <u>before</u> seeing them, nor withheld payment until healing is achieved, I have always paid when I check out <u>after</u> seeing the doctor. I guess they're a bit lenient on forcing me to pay up front because I've got such a good record of not walking out without paying.

My delayed, yet always paid, co-pay remittance must somehow mitigate the first edict for me at least. Oh, but without consideration of any possible mitigation, the second rule was truly mystifying: **If you fail to pay your co-pay, there will be a $5.00 additional co-pay which must be paid BEFORE you see the doctor at your next scheduled appointment.**

What happened to number one? How could there be a "next scheduled appointment" if I had not seen the doctor the first time. After all, Rule #1 specifically excludes seeing the doctor if I failed to remit the co-pay <u>first</u>. The projector in my mental viewing room illuminated as I imagined the doctor's office as a game board. Wearing a pewter top hat, I envisioned the nurse calling me out of the waiting room. I counted my steps along the way to Room #2, just past Water Works…the drinking fountain. Abruptly the nurse halts my progress. "You failed to stop at GO! You now owe five more dollars. Return directly to GO. DO NOT stop at Scales, Blood Pressure Testing or Temperature Probe. Pay the Banker your Co-pay, plus $5 penalty."

My sight returned from the viewing room to peruse the 3rd rule. Believe it or not, it stated that it was not their responsibility to know the amount of my co-pay.

Hold on there, Quick Draw. Baba Looey's got some thinkin' fer ya. Let's see…if they don't know what my co-pay is, how would they know if I'd paid it in full and thus be allowed to see the doctor?

Oh, I get it. They know, but they aren't about to tell me and lose out on a chance to gain the penalty money. If I shortchange them this time, even if by accident, next time I'll owe the $5 penalty plus the next co-pay or I don't see the doctor.

I quickly re-read the rules.

Pay co-pay or you don't see the doctor.

If you don't pay correctly, next time you owe $5 plus your next co-pay or you don't see the doctor.

Co-pay amount is my responsibility.

What's missing? What about the imbalance if I pay the wrong amount? There was no mention of when I had to pay the amount that I shorted them the first time.

When I mentioned to Sue that I would bring this matter up when they returned from lunch, Sue recommended I just sit down and stop reading. I guess my history with such ponderings is not good. As the receptionist began sliding open her glass window, Sue jumped up, "Just don't pay any attention to him. I think his fever is affecting his mind."

Now, here's the real kicker. When I came out <u>after</u> seeing the doctor, I tried to pay my co-pay. They advised me that I had overpaid the last time, so they would deduct that difference from my co-pay this time. I paused a moment, considering whether I should suggest that they owe <u>me</u> a $5 penalty for allowing my overpayment last time.

Must be Sue's intuitive 6th sense told her where my mind was going. She quickly ushered me out of the office before I could utter a single word. Next time though, I'll certainly try to balance the books to the semantics of the rules.

QUESTION OF THE DAY:

What went wrong with Preparations A through G?

Not that I actually needed Preparation H, but going into a clinic to have a colonoscopy performed, I did notice an advertisement that caused me to contemplate the history of this medication.

9

Diversion Excursion

Tuesday, I had a doctor's appointment. Actually it was a procedure; namely, a colonoscopy. You know, one of those every-5-year "screenings" for 55 and older folks. I have no idea why they would call it a "screening." By the time you starve yourself for a day then chug-a-lug a couple Fleet phosposodas, there isn't a whole lot left to screen.

Anyway, the entire day before, food consumption was prohibited. Such a proscription for me is like telling a cow, "Yesterday's cud's all ya get today." Now for cows, and a grazer like me, that's a huge sacrifice. I normally can't make 30 minutes without munching on something. Fasting 30 hours could cause atrophy of my jaw muscles.

I chomped on gum just for the chewing sensation. I even thought about accidentally swallowing my double wad of bubble gum so my stomach wouldn't suffer total withdrawal. Then I got this hideous visualization of Double Bubble on the colonoscopy scope and spit out the gum.

So, now I've been off my feed bag for a day. Sue says she thinks I need a distraction. She proposes that rather than wait until just before I have to be at the clinic, we could run a few errands…do some shopping. "Time will go by faster," she suggested, "and it should take your mind off of not eating. Maybe you won't be quite so miserable."

Oh, sure, she sounded sympathetic to my plight. BUT… First stop: Walmart. Guess what's just inside the entrance of Walmart. In case you don't remember, the Snack Bar with fans blowing greasy vapors into the aisle. So much for diverting my thoughts from eating.

And we didn't even buy anything at Walmart. Sue said they didn't have what she was looking for. How could Walmart not have something? Nevertheless, into the store a hundred feet past the diner and back out. Free aroma therapy…no purchase necessary.

Well, that certainly distracted me. If it weren't for the Boy Scout troop tying my stomach in square knots, I'd surely have forgotten about food altogether.

You know, sometimes I wonder why I let Sue go with me to these appointments. No doubt her intentions are loving and she thinks she's doing what's best. There are times, though, when her train of thought gets derailed. Around the corner from the Walmart fiasco, Sue jumped the tracks again. Ah, yes…into Kroger we rolled.

How could Sue possibly consider a grocery store as a great diversion from hunger pangs? Hey, walking by the meat counter wasn't tough for her. She'd just finished a banana—which incidentally can fill a car with aroma faster than a mirror-hung pine tree in the car. Yet banana vapors do not stimulate my appetite quite so much as the sight of red meat. If my saliva glands had not dried up hours ago, I'd surely have drooled a puddle right there in Aisle Four. Oh, boy, how the time was just flying by with these shopping trip distractions!

Fortunately, with shopping completed, it was time to head for the clinic. Upon exit from Kroger, I noticed she'd purchased a snack pack. All is forgiven and I remark, "Gee, hon, how sweet of you. These will sure hit the spot after my procedure."

"I doubt there will be much left," Sue apologized. "I've got such a long wait for them to finish the colonoscopy and for you to come out from under the drugs." It was bad enough that she teased me with sight of these delightful morsels. Then she opened them. Do you have any idea how much aroma wafts out of a package of Ritz Bits in a matter of seconds?

Somehow she survived my daggered glare and got me to the clinic. The prep nurse not only advised me of what was to happen during my visit to the clinic, she also presented me with a list of *do's and don'ts*, which I'd have to follow after the procedure. One was "No strenuous activity the balance of the day." I asked why this simple procedure would keep me from playing softball that evening.

"Well, sir," she replied. "It's because the drugs you'll be given might cause you to become dizzy during the game and possibly fall."

Sue quickly interjected, "That's no big deal. He wasn't on drugs before last week's game and fell anyway."

Is there anyone out there reading this who'd volunteer to drive me to my next colonoscopy?

QUESTION OF THE DAY:

Why is it that we fill in the blanks when we fill out a form?

Prepositions like in and out may be defined as a preface to a noun which modifies a verb. For me, in and out was what I hoped would happen when we went to Urgent Care for Sue's injured finger.

10

A Question of Pertinence

"So what brings you here today?" came the perfunctory question from the receptionist.

"Well, you see," Sue began. "Every year, for Christmas, we put up a Dickens Village. I know it's really early, but we're about to go to Disney World and the last time we put it off until we got back, we never did get it up. So, anyway, we were getting ready to put up Dickens in the bookcases, and Ed had painted this really nice backdrop. It isn't a real work of art, but, you know, good enough for a miniature village skyline. Anyway, the backdrop had to go behind…"

As Sue recounted the incident of her injury, I couldn't help but wonder why women provide so much extraneous information. The question was simple. Why are you here? It had purpose. So, why was Sue taking such a divergent path to satisfy that purpose? I would have simply answered; "Smashed my finger."

Ah, but it was Sue's finger…and her story. Who am I to suggest she cut the narrative short before she bled out. After all, typically my stories are filled with enough hot air to float a life raft, so a little tolerance was in order—despite my urge to speed up the process.

Maybe Sue wasn't dripping blood all over the floor, but there was a reason we'd come to URGENT CARE and it wasn't for story time. Besides, the opening question wasn't even posed by a doctor or even the triage nurse. It was just the receptionist's cordial greeting. Eventually though, Sue got to the punch line that her finger had a significant cut that needed attention.

"Here, please fill out these forms and sign all these releases."

Forms, without much doubt, written by a woman like Sue. Talk about extraneous information. "List all surgeries and hospital stays: ." Sue had not had one such incident since giving birth to Kim. Other than the gradient comparison of childbirth pain to her finger's current scream for relief, the relevance of listing surgeries seemed a bit superfluous to me.

And, that was just the first blank to fill in...or out...whatever. Just get it done. The pages were full of seemingly irrelevant queries. Sure, most of them had medical overtones, but why not just a one-liner, "Where does it hurt?" That simple question has worked brilliantly for a bazillion mothers checking on their child's injury.

Oh, but that wasn't the end of verbiage overkill. Next we saw the triage nurse. As luck would have it, this particular nurse is a friend of Sue's aforementioned daughter, Kim. Despite now being in the examining room, no examining was in progress. They were talking about Kim's new job and the potential hazards of working at a prison.

Helllllloooooo. Injury! ...pain, ...blood, ...ah, maybe you could take a quick peek at Sue's finger.

Not yet. "Sue, would you step up on the scale, please."

What was that for...tare weight? Were they going to bill us on how much their bandaging weighed?

Even with a plethora of arguably impertinent information Sue had recorded on the patient questionnaire, plus the medical data recorded on the nurse's form, and Kim's new job thoroughly diagnosed, the nurse then launched into her own inquisition. "Do you feel safe at home?"

Sue deliberated her answer for a moment before answering, "With him?"

They both chuckled, yet it was painfully true. The injury we were seeking treatment for was directly the result of my mishandling a shelf which ended its downward travel by sandwiching Sue's finger against the next shelf down.

Finally, the nurse unwrapped my hasty bandaging and went to get the doctor. Oh, no; the physician was a woman. Sorry for such a chauvinistic judgment, but, look it up—gossip is a feminine gender noun...Middle English.

Bias aside, I was sure we were in for another round of extraneous information sharing between women. Especially when her greeting to Sue was, "And, what brings you here today?"

But, alas, even as she spoke those words, she was inspecting Sue's finger. Her query was almost rhetorical. No more long stories or irrelevant information to document. At last, Sue's finger was the focal point.

Examination revealed the shelf had hit the middle finger with sufficient force to actually rupture the skin in 3 places. X-rays revealed an open fracture about a quarter inch from the tip. The doctor wrapped the wounds and told Sue to keep it dry and elevated. "You can't cook tonight," ordered the doctor.

"Well, neither can he!" Sue retorted.

Wow, that was certainly pertinent! It was not verbose, chatty or fraught with extraneous information…succinct, relevant and, though a bit blunt, very true. Fortunately, the injury was to Sue's right hand. She's left-handed, so she could still call a restaurant for reservations.

QUESTION OF THE DAY:

Why aren't cookies called bakies?

I do not belong in the kitchen. When I was in training to help an automotive mechanic, I could ask questions and he'd answer them without mocking me. My asking Sue questions in the kitchen is bound to elicit exasperated sighs. Yes, I do know what is involved in the processes of both baking and cooking and that is why I will never understand the rationale for a "baked" disc of dough to be called a "cookie."

11

Three-Handed Cooking

I mentioned a couple a weeks ago that Sue had broken her finger. Part of the doctor's orders at that time were that she was not to soak the bandaged wound. Getting it wet was acceptable, but no dishwashing.

The surgeon went on to advise Sue to refrain from grabbing tightly, or squeezing. Whew! I was sure glad to hear that. No squeezing would rule out choking me as is often Sue's temptation. Furthermore, "…no lifting, pushing and shoving. Especially gripping, pushing and shoving."

I suggested to the doctor his directive meant no shopping. Sue understood it as no cooking or housework. The doctor agreed with Sue and further stipulated, "For a couple years, at least." It's a good thing insurance is paying his bill, 'cause he wouldn't get a dime out of me for ruling out housekeeping tasks.

Actually, it really didn't seem like a big concern for me. I used to wash dishes at a restaurant during my college days and I'm quite capable of putting together a few simple meals while Sue recovers.

Unfortunately, prior to Sue's injury, she had volunteered to fix a meal for our church's mid-week activities. So, Wednesday, just about the time I contemplated whether to fix tuna sandwiches or soup and crackers, Sue exclaims, "We need to get started making chili."

Suddenly, my simple lunch turned into dinner for thirty. But, hey, what could be so tough in making a pot of chili and a few dozen cookies? After all, Sue would be there to coach me. Besides, this isn't exactly new. I've helped Sue cook and bake lots of times.

However, it turns out, my helping Sue is a whole lot different than her helping me. Maybe two heads are better than one, but two heads operating three hands make for a tangled mess.

She was constantly reaching around, across and between my arms with her good hand. I'd be stirring and she'd reach from behind me to add a cup of something. Whoosh, slop... half of it on the counter.

I'm tellin' ya, when the Head Chef's brains are in a different body than the Chief Cook, there's more trouble brewin' than chili. It's a miracle we didn't get hot sauce in the chocolate chip cookies. Guaranteed, nobody would notice the chips in the chili. Wow, do they melt quickly!

Those times when I helped her in the kitchen, effectively she would stand at the counter while I would dash about, "get this for me...pour that in...open a can of...I need you to..." But this time I had to do all that fetchin' plus slice, dice, stir, brown, simmer...AND wash dishes.

As I washed the cooking pans and utensils, a startling revelation came to me. I may have discovered a rare health hazard right in our own kitchen.

As I put a cookie sheet in the sink, I noticed a strange discolored pattern on the bottom. "What's this on the bottom of the cookie sheet?" I asked innocently.

"Tape." Sue quickly replied.

"Tape? You leave tape on the bottom of the cookie sheet?"

"Yeah. It won't come off. It's baked on."

"But isn't that dangerous? There's gotta be some adverse chemicals vaporizing off of that tape into the oven air every time you bake."

"Don't be silly, Ed. That tape's been on there for years."

"Oh, my…then you've been slowly poisoning me for a long time, huh? Now I'm on to you."

"What are you talking about, anyway?"

"The other day, I got an e-mail warning about residual poisoning."

"Residual poisoning?" Sue guffawed a skeptical response.

"Yup. Some woman's dog licked its paws and got residual poisoning after walking across floors cleaned by Swifter."

"It's **Swiffer®**, not <u>swiffer</u>."

"I know…I know…<u>Swift</u>er would be faster acting; Swiffer is a slooow, agonizing death. No doubt, the extreme oven heat activates emissions from the glue on this tape. I'm betting it is cumulative, like mercury. It's my civic duty to get the message out about this potential medical hazard. I've gotta warn all my friends…or at least 10 of them and hopefully get some wonderful prize in return."

Consider yourself warned….

QUESTION OF THE DAY:

If you are not "pretty close", are you ugly far?

This **? of the day** was concocted as I was checking in for an appointment at a local hospital's Neo Natal Clinic. I mentioned, "I'll bet you get about one guy a year here." She replied, "Pretty close."

12

Why me, why here?

Okay, can someone tell me why my medical maladies so often lead me to women's clinics? A couple of years ago, I spent the night in a hospital's Woman's Care Unit following my sinus surgery. Just what link there might be between my nose and the maternity ward is beyond my comprehension.

Now, this morning my doctor once again sent me into a sanctum of women's care. He scheduled me to visit the Sparrow Neo Natal Clinic. Why?

No..., not why was I there. Ultrasound...neo natal...makes sense. But why send a man to a woman's clinic for anything. Isn't there a men's clinic that has an ultrasound machine? Really! Set one up in a garage somewhere. Hang some tools on the wall. Put some sawdust in bowls for aroma, tune in ESPN and set out a pot of day-old coffee on a bench. Yeah, that's an environment where a man could be comfortable.

Women's clinics are not set up for men. Floral arrangements, latte, soothing Muzak™. Transcendent ambiance for many patients, but me?... Lemme hear the roar of a V-8 while I wait.

It's not just the atmosphere of a Neo Natal Clinic that's a bit out of my comfort zone. I was the first patient on the docket. Nevertheless, I still had to wait a half hour. Women who go there are used to waiting. They're on a nine-month schedule. What's another half hour.

But I hadn't eaten since supper the night before. And that meal had to be fat free. How long does non-fat anything stay in a man's stomach. I wanted to get in and get out and be off to breakfast. I was hungry. My stomach was making enough noise to distort the ultrasound. Not only did I have to wait, they didn't have "Sports Illustrated", "Car & Driver" or "Outdoor Life". I'm tellin' ya, "Babies Home Journal" didn't captivate my attention for long.

Then, I finally get the call. The technician…a woman, of course, led me down the hall. It was lined with **Vital Pregnancy Practice** posters, a few warm, fuzzy, mother and child pictures, plus an array of pretty pastel paintings with distinctly feminine counsel superimposed.

There was not even one picture of a grizzled old man battling a lunker bass. Not a single male-identity item visible anywhere. And every attendant we passed did a double take. They seemed as surprised at a man's presence as I was at the absence of masculinity in the corridor. When I mentioned this to my technician, she admitted, "We don't get very many men here."

"Oh, Really?" I remarked with a hint of sarcasm. "It can't be that unusual for a man to have his gall bladder scoped?"

"No. I scope men often. Just not here."

"Ahhh, so tell me...," I suggestively inquired, "where do you scope men?"

"Ohhhh, not like that. I also work at the other radiology lab here at the hospital. I must say, I'm not sure why your doctor didn't send you there."

That made two of us wondering why my doctor sent me to a women's clinic. Come to think of it, my personal physician didn't have any influence on *where* I should have the ultrasound. Rather, it was his scheduling nurse. Ah, ha...I shall have to get even with her for this. Of course, there's the distinct possibility that this was a case of her getting even with me. Maybe, I'd better let it go.

QUESTION OF THE DAY:

Do you take a laxative with any regularity?

This question was actually posed by an MSU Doctoral student. I love working with these young people who so earnestly study to be doctors, yet struggle so often with wording their investigating inquiries.

13

Annual Physicals

Would you believe I've spent the last three days having an annual physical? Yup, it took six doctors three days to give me a comprehensive physical. Okay, so maybe they weren't exactly doctors yet, and I wasn't exactly *myself* either.

The truth, exactly—the doctors were student practitioners in Michigan State University's College of Human Medicine. I was portraying a fictional person for the exams. Though my symptoms and medical history are scripted, I am given some liberties in how I answer a student's inquiry.

Some liberties, yet not carte blanche improvisation. These encounters are much more than role-playing. The student's physical exam of me is coincidentally an exam of their competency at this stage of their education. The stakes are high and so is their stress level. Often, I try to relax their tension with humor. Generally, that tactic works fairly well.

A student had been firing a battery of standard questions with a gaze much like a deer in headlights. He knew the questions cold. Similarly his facial expression was nearly frozen and his stilted phrasing was a bit chilly. I thought a little thawing humor might warm him up a bit.

After asking, "Are you taking any prescription medications?", he posed the next procedural inquiry: "Are you on any drugs?"

To break his frozen string of questions, I decided to take his inquiry quite literally and replied, "Is it that obvious?"

"No, no, I didn't mean at this moment. I mean," he stammered, "…like yesterday. Do you take any recreational drugs regularly."

"Does Viagra qualify as recreational?"

"Oh, no, I am so sorry," now, quite embarrassed. "It's just a standard question for an exam like this."

"It's just the way you phrased it that made me suspicious. Then the answer is no, I haven't been on drugs since my hippie days. But…oh, man…did I get spaced out a few times back in the day" — which incidentally was within my scripted character that day.

Even that seemed to increase his tension. I could see that my humor was ill-fated with him. I almost wished I had a "downer" in my pocket to give him.

I think this, almost mandatory, inquiry about a patient's possible use of illicit drugs is one where students often stumble over phrasing. It's not easy to pry into a patient's personal life without offending them. Other examples of ill-worded drug-user inquiries and my replies:

"Do you now, or have you ever used illegal drugs?"

I suspiciously looked around the room. "Are you actually a cop and this is being taped?"

"Do you take any drugs without a prescription?"

"You mean like stealing them?"

"Have you ever used illegal street drugs?"

"Wow! You mean some street drugs are legal?"

Yes, I know my responses were really being nit-picky on wording. Yet, they did often alleviate a student's anxiety.

It is amazing how often humor is a great equalizer. Even though most of the students came into the room a bit apprehensive, I believe the chuckles I was able to elicit from them soon calmed the atmosphere. It was a great experience for me as an actor, humorist, and educator. Besides, I passed six complete physicals.

QUESTION OF THE DAY:

If time heals all wounds, how come I can still see my belly button?

Some would say that "bonding" begins through the umbilical cord. In a way, my granddaughter's and my respective belly buttons exemplify our grand-paternal bonding. We each had navel hernias repaired a day apart. With such mutual bonding, it's no wonder she could hardly wait to tell me about her first experience with the tooth fairy.

(14)

Tooth Fairy

"Papa, Papa!!! Look!" exclaimed Amara, racing toward me.

She hadn't bothered to even unzip her coat…or close the front door either. Opening the door was a necessity, but for a purpose-driven seven-year-old, closing it isn't even an afterthought. Full steam ahead, arms outstretched, mouth open wide…she resembled a fighter jet sucking in air through her nose-cone intake. An intake that had a chip in its cowl.

"You lost your tooth, didn't you?" I responded, matching her glee.

"No, I didn't," came her hands-on-hips retort.

"Wellllll, if you didn't lose it, where'd it go? It's not in your mouth anymore."

"I didn't lose it. I gave it to the tooth fairy."

"You did? How much did you get?"

"A dollar."

A dollar! She got a whole dollar. Inflation is rampant even in fairyland. I was lucky to get a dime. And, if I didn't make a public proclamation when a new tooth went under the pillow, I got nothin'.

What... Must there be some ceremonial liturgy with accompanying parent gods as I place my tooth on the sacrificial altar beneath my pillow? Is there a criteria of 'goodness' required by the fickle tooth fairy? In my boyish mind, I only needed to stick a tooth under the pillow to receive a stipend. Okay, so maybe wash it off first, but that's it. Under the pillow... money in the mornin'.

Then one night it happened. Lying in bed, wiggling a tooth that flapped when I talked, out it came. Not wishing to incur the wrath of the parent gods for getting out of bed after prayers, I simply deposited the tooth beneath my pillow. My plea of penance was accompanied by a petition for great wealth. Well, at least enough to afford a Payday®.

In the morning I peeled back the pillow shroud of the tooth fairy altar. No tooth on the altar linens. Nor was there any money. Not even a penny for a single piece of candy. That's when I stopped believing in the tooth fairy. It did not mitigate my lost faith in fairyland to find my tooth stuck to the underside of my pillow. Spirits are not bound by human senses.

Eventually, I suppose, tooth fairies forget. I wonder if it's significant that fairies are female. Elves, not fairies, work with Santa. Santa and his elves do not forget Christmas. Fantasy males forget nothing. I guess fantasyland is the exact opposite of reality. Human males forget everything. But, until the tooth fairy slips up, she is very real to Amara.

"Papa, I saw her when she gave me the dollar."

"Oh, really. I thought the tooth fairy came while you were sleeping."

"Yeah. But, she said she was sorry she woke me up."

As you might imagine, I thought the ploy had been exposed on Amara's very first tooth. The tooth fairy had not been cautious enough.

"And she was beautiful," Amara continued. "She had on a red and orange dress. Yeah, and purple shoes…" Now Amara was in the grasp of a crescendo of excitement. "…and black hair and red eyes and a crown and a wand and everything."

"Wow! You actually woke up and saw the tooth fairy?"

"Yeah. But she said she wouldn't leave me my dollar if I didn't close my eyes and go back to sleep."

"So…you got a dollar, huh? Are you going to share it with Papa?"

The look in Amara's eyes told me she had returned from fairyland and was back to reality. The tooth was Amara's and so was the dollar. Papa was now the one fanaticizing with the sharing suggestion. Fantasies are a wonderful thing. Both for little girls and Papas.

QUESTION OF THE DAY:

If you crossed poison ivy and a four-leaf clover, would you get a rash of good luck?

Although experimentation with crossbreeding plants has many limitations, mating my medications in milk — prior to their intimate mingling in my stomach — intrigued me.

15

Medicinal Experimentation

I just finished breakfast. Fried eggs, sausage, cracked wheat toast… hopefully the fiber will wrap itself around the cholesterol and drag it out of my system.

Hey, before you get on my case about all the fat and cholesterol, take note. I also drank some pomegranate juice and green tea. Gotta have those antioxidants. I crave fats and cholesterol, so I make sure I eat enough "good stuff" to offset the reportedly negative effects of what I enjoy.

I also take a host of pills every day. Some of them are after-the-fact medications intended to quell certain maladies that have snuck past before-the-fact pills I take as preventatives. Let's face it, even huge doses of Vitamin C cannot screen out someone's sneeze in your face.

The majority of my pills are, categorically, wellness promoters. I take them, but don't really have much confidence. I lost a lot of wellness confidence when my adolescent breakfasts of Wheaties did not make me a champion. Humph! I didn't even make the team most of the time. Not to mention that Wonder Bread failed to build my body strength in 7 out of 8 advertised ways. Big feet was all I got. Big, clumsy feet.

Contrary to my uncertainties, I take some pills just on the chance of improving regularity, sharpening my vision—which Wonder Bread did not—and trapping beaver-like cholesterol in my bloodstream before dams are built.

There's also a bunch of pills in my daily regimen which are like scab labor to a strike. I have a long-standing boycott of green legumes. Most notably, lima beans. Especially when combined with mushy corn slop…otherwise known as succotash. Oh, my…just speaking that word gags me.

On the table this morning, my pills formed a veritable rainbow arching around my bowl. As I contemplated this lovely palate of pills, I could not help but recall an experiment I conducted.

On a typically routine morning a while back, I had a similar arrangement of various colored medications to take after breakfast. On that day, my wonderment about what color these pills might develop in my stomach got the best of me. I first resupplied my cereal bowl with some milk.

Then, I selected an azure tablet from the array on the table and floated it gently in the milk. My wonderment was rewarded as the pill began to dissolve almost immediately. Oh, such a pretty hue of blue. Distinctly royal-looking. Ever so gently, I stirred the milk—an artistic stir, creating a delightful swirl. Certainly lovely. But it needed enhancement. I searched the color palate next to my bowl.

Hmmm, there were a pair of lavender capsules. I let them slide down the edge of the bowl. Unlike the blue tablet, these sunk. With imaginative anticipation, I leaned over my bowl hoping for color to erupt from the depths of the milk. Nothing. No doubt they were time-release capsules.

Back to the pill pile. Oh, look…a red and clear capsule full of pink and white granules. Likely, another time-release capsule which I felt an urgency to outwit. I twisted the capsule open and dumped the contents into the mix. Whoa! Instant dots of tint. Actually, they were floating not dissolving, but it was still quite appealing.

I was on a roll. Into the mix went three, instant acting, brilliant yellow monstrosities. Ah, yes. That was more like it. A yellow haze began to permeate the solution. I must admit, I was a bit disappointed at the loss of gloss.

Actually, it was more than just the loss of brightness in my colorific creation. The blue inexorably dispersed from its delightful swirl, the dots of tint either sunk or diffused into the resultant tarnished-gold solution, and even the lavender capsules finally dissolved and erupted like an undersea volcano. My surrealistic art slowly—and irreverently—turned to black.

It wasn't just the color change which disturbed me. There was a scum forming. Yuck. I should never have allowed my childish mind such freedom that morning.

My mental movie of that day went to black also. Today, after enjoying a breakfast of sunny-side-up eggs, I ponder the pile of pills next to my pomegranate juice. I wonder what artistic creation is about to develop in my stomach. I wonder...did Renoir ever paint *La Noir Enthousiasme.*

QUESTION OF THE DAY:

We can "give out," "give in" and "give up" ...What happened to "give down"?

Commonly used phrasing, such as "give up" with no correlative phrase "give down," has always perplexed me. However, in the following experiences — without regard to "give" — the "up" and "down" arrows on my examination table's foot controls seemed to create bewilderment for a few medical students.

16

Not in Control

I realize doctors must go to school a long time just to get their license to practice. However, I now know they need a little more time to practice some mechanical skills, too. Simple things, like learning the fine points of manipulating the examination table.

I'm sure I've mentioned I am an SP (Standardized Patient) for the medical colleges at Michigan State University. This week I was a patient for cardiac exams. Normally, my heart would not have given them much practical experience in discerning "heart trouble". However, I think a few of them found my heart to be skipping beats while they were trying to operate the exam table.

I don't know if the table in my examination room was new or old, technology-wise, but it most certainly was new to them. It was automated by a foot bar with up (↑) and down (↓) arrows in five categories. BACK, HEAD, FOOT, LIFT, and TILT. Four letters each.

When a student enters my room, the table is set at a 30-degree angle. Between students, I establish the table at that angle. It is quite simply accomplished with the foot activated pedal—HEAD ⬆. At the onset of one of my exams, a distinctly diminutive gal remarked that she needed to lower my head.

Lower as in ⬇. Head as in H-E-A-D. In spite of her intentions, she apparently confused the arrows as well as mistaking LIFT for HEAD. Eeeengh, the LIFT motor whirred and UP went the table. The entire table, not just the HEAD.

She mumbled something which was distinctly neither medical nor layman terminology. Then, apologetically exclaimed, "I don't think I did that right."

At least she was listening in class when the professor advised to not understate the obvious to a patient. She stepped back, peered down at the activation bar on the floor and tried again ...eeeenghhh, ...up some more. Her learning curve was still going down whilst I was going up.

Another frustrated mumble and a shuffle of her feet. Eeeengh. Finally, the HEAD was indeed going down. Despite her vertically-challenged stature, her foot was large enough to activate both the LIFT and TILT motors simultaneously. About the time my upper torso leveled to my legs, the vertical rise of the entire table had reached max elevation.

Did I mention she was diminutive? I glanced in her direction. We were now face to face...me prone, she upright.

With a sign of relief, she asked, "Well, now. Are you comfortable?"

"I guess you could say I'm a bit high," I responded with a chuckle to try to settle her nerves.

All things considered, she managed to complete the exam with remarkable poise. Of course, she had to walk around the table to listen to the left side of my chest. However, checking my knee reflexes did not require her to bend down.

Just to allay any thoughts that I might be sexist, mechanical ineptitudes have likewise been apparent with some of the guys.

When the exam table is in the 30-degree position, it approximates a recliner. As the French would say, a *chaise longue*. The French *longue* sounds so much more comfortable than the Americanized lounge—not to mention a French *chaise* is upholstered, not plastic webbing. With either pronunciation, a body at rest upon such a long chair has its feet supported while gently bent at the hip in a very relaxed attitude. Unlike the French longue, an American medical exam table may support a body head to foot, yet it has pivot points where my 6'4" frame does not. Attitude adjustment; mandatory.

That is to say, for me, it is necessary to extend the table's leg support if I am asked to recline, because, with my hip, even at the uppermost juncture of the table, the "seat" portion is much shorter than the distance from my hip to my knees.

During one of my exams, a young man stated correctly that he needed me to be at 30 degrees rather than sitting up straight. He asked me to lie back against the table—which I had pre-set at 30-degrees. I did as he requested while he moved to the table control pedals.

Beats me why so many students likes the TILT button. Unfortunately, he failed to extend the leg support portion of the table before activating TILT.

Let's see... hygienic, smooth, exam table paper... vinyl upholstery... feet down...TILT. A toboggan at 30 degrees on hard packed snow would not have slid down the slope any faster than did my 250-pound body on the exam table's paper sled.

I can't help but wonder if Michigan State should institute a mechanical aptitude requirement for Med-school.

QUESTION OF THE DAY:

If you want someone to clearly see something, why would you run it by them?

I suppose we might run an idea by our friends so that they won't clearly see it. Maybe it wasn't intended to deceive me, but a friend did run something by me quite quickly — which I clearly "saw" too late.

17

Helping Out

One of the things Sue and I appreciate about retirement is the freedom to help a friend in need. Often that happens when someone needs transportation for a medical procedure. There is great satisfaction in giving someone a ride when they are instructed not to drive. Of course, sometimes that satisfaction is somewhat obscured as the event unfolds.

A friend mentioned she needed a ride to and from such a procedure. I shall call her Martha and she was about to have out-patient surgery. Considering that Martha has no spouse and shares her apartment with an unlicensed guinea pig, she needed someone to drive her to the hospital and back home again.

She assured me the surgery would last about an hour, and recovery… maybe another hour. "We'll be home by noon," was her estimate. So, I consented to transport her.

Martha continued, "Can you pick me up at 6:00?" I should have gotten a hint of pending problems when the math didn't quite work.

Noon, minus one hour of recovery, one hour of surgery and one hour of travel does not equal my alarm being set for 5 a.m. But, I had already committed my assistance, so I agreed to pick her up at 6 a.m.

Check-in at the hospital went quite smoothly. Well, all except pre-op briefing. Once again, hints of potential complications.

Martha must have emphasized her aversion to anesthetics a half-dozen times. First to the triage nurse, then an RN, the PA, the surgeon, the anesthesiologist's aide and finally, the anesthetist himself. I think Martha even mentioned it to the janitor who happened to sweep past her doorway. All gave confident assurance they would only sedate her to minimal levels of subconscious as well as give her the best anti-nausea medications.

Personally, I thought Martha was being a bit paranoid about a little analgesic in the IV. I mean, this was arthroscopic surgery, not a heart transplant. They only needed her to be groggy, not comatose.

"You'll be fine," Sue and I assured her as we headed for the waiting lounge.

An hour went by and I expected to hear we could go in to see Martha in recovery. We'd heard she was out of surgery, but nothing more. Two hours passed as did the four cups of coffee from my bladder. At three hours, my solar plexus was convulsing like the eruption of sun spots. I need food, but can't afford to miss the surgeon's visit to the waiting room.

But, no surgeon appeared. Hour four and I almost expected to see the Chaplain. What was wrong? A few holes in the knee, a little scraping and… *"Hey, wake up Martha…it's over."*

Instead, Sue was waking me up; I had dozed off. A nurse was coming our way. She advised us that Martha was not feeling well, but we could go back to see her.

We entered Martha's recovery room. She looked like death was imminent. She wasn't just pale. She must have sneezed into a powdered sugar doughnut. Television corpses have more color than she did. Not feeling well was a GROSS understatement—with capitalization warranted. She wasn't just a little queasy. She looked like her bed had just completed two barrel rolls and a loopty-loop of a corkscrew coaster.

We tried to be sympathetic and encouraging to her. She was not encouraged. She told us the nausea was <u>exactly</u> what had happened with her last arthroscopic surgery. Hmmm, a significant detail she failed to mention to me during preliminary negotiations for transportation.

With her recovery entering into its fifth hour, they decided to admit her for overnight observation. I was relieved—and not just from the responsibility of taking her home. I was getting a bit woozy just observing her.

A simple, out-patient surgery, I had thought would take but a few hours, had been prolonged to a whole day. All because of an adverse reaction to the anesthesia…admitted by Martha…after-the-fact, as predictable.

I told Martha, "The next time you go in for surgery, save money… cancel the anesthesiologist. I'll smack you in the head with a baseball bat and give you some Vicodin. You probably won't get home any sooner, but you won't be nauseous from the anesthetic either."

QUESTION OF THE DAY:

Is the extent of laryngitis measured in hoarsepower?

It was not laryngitis that necessitated an appointment with my dentist. In effect though, I wasn't able to talk much during the visit.

18

Dental Work

"So, how'd it go," Sue inquired as she greeted me with a kiss. Normally, a kiss is an exciting reception. But coming home from the dentist?...not so much exciting as bizarre. Kind of a Dali surrealism with my lips being only on one side. I got half a kiss. On the other side, the kiss seemed to be sliding off my face.

I love going to the dentist. Some people do drugs to alter their senses. Me, I prefer Novocain. I can hardly wait to get home from the dentist to slurry a mouthful of water. Wild, maaan...farrrr out. It's like... it's there... but it isn't.

It's even strangely delightful to look in the mirror and watch myself drool, with no sensation of the escaping liquid. Next time I'm going to ask the dentist if she'll give me a little nitrous oxide as I'm about to leave for home. A silly soprano giggle would surely top off the experience.

I've had three dentists. All of them have made my dental experiences rather pleasant...all things considered. Each one of them has been enjoyably unique in their demeanor, yet all three about the same in practice. They greet you congenially, usually punctuated with their personal brand of levity. They will then fill my mouth with tools and ask something like, "Take any trips lately?"

Now, I realize that question could be answered simply with eh-heh—which could be transliterated either yes or no. Not that I believe the dentist is actually expecting a travelogue, but I am addicted to verbosity. Considering, by that time, my tongue is numb and propped up with cotton wads. Who can voice anything intelligible without the use of their tongue…not to mention a vacuum cleaner hose draped over their lip?

My current dental health administrator has state-of-the-art equipment. She's got cable TV for me to view—if only that miserable spotlight wasn't glaring at me. She has all the latest bells and whistles available to dentistry. Actually, more bells than whistles. Just about everything she sticks in my mouth rings the "done" bell eventually.

I'm going to suggest one more 21st century item to her. I'm thinking she should provide me with an E-tablet displaying four multiple-choice questions to choose from. I could pick one, then *swipe* my answers on the keyboard.

Of course, considering her attention should be in my mouth, not reading the tablet, it would be better if her assistant would verbalize what I've typed on the screen. Oh, wait, the assistant's maneuvering the super-sucker, so that won't work, either.

Actually, I think they already utilize the best solution. Between the two of them, they carry on a conversation that they consider appropriate for me to listen in on, yet doesn't necessarily require my response. As long as the dentist isn't drilling, their dialogue does tend to distract me.

Because the technology of my hearing aids automatically adjust the loudest sound down to my comfort level. I clearly and distinctly hear the drill excavating my tooth. Their conversation is distant and muted. Somewhat like a gagged heroine pleading for help from deep within a well. For me, trying to hear anything beyond the disintegration of enamel is akin to unaided ears understanding a guy running his mouth and a jack hammer.

I don't mind, though. Their voices are gentle and their conversation almost melodious. Inarticulate, yet great background music. It lulls me as she grinds away on a tooth.

When she finishes, I am grateful neither of them ask for my opinion on anything they've discussed.

They are very sensitive that way. In fact, I'd say they have the same sensitivity toward my insensitive mouth as I do. One of them invariably asks if I would like to rinse my mouth. Just like me in front of the mirror at home, they seem to enjoy the perverse pleasure from watching me drool.

QUESTION OF THE DAY:

Do ghosts drink evaporated milk?

Seeing ghosts, lapsing into aberration and experiencing paranoia are certainly not laughable matters. I do not intend this story to belittle such experiences. None-the-less, my portrayal of a paranoid individual did turn out to be a bit humorous.

19

They're Out There

The Place: MSU's Learning and Assessment Center (LAC)

The Occasion: Standardized Patient-Training for a Case to assess medical students for proficiency in psychiatric evaluation.

The Case: Paranoia.

In preparation for viewing a video tape of this case from last year, the LAC staff-trainer pointed toward me and advised the other trainees, "We are going to watch Ed for a few minutes. He is a perfect example of someone who needs further psychiatric evaluation."

This probably does not come as a particular surprise to most of you. Before you call to see if I was admitted to the nut ward, I'll remind you that a Standardized Patient portrays an imaginary character—and in this particular case, imagining things.

The staff-trainer called on me as an example because I was reprising a character I portrayed a year ago. Apparently, I was quite convincing as

William Kahn—a paranoid, delusional individual who thinks "they" are out to steal him blind.

I gladly admit, I truly enjoy being an SP. It offers me a wonderful opportunity to act while providing a practical, non-threatening, experience for medical students. It also provides many interesting, often humorous, interactions with them.

For example: After an exemplary introduction by a student about to evaluate William Kahn, she began her investigative interview with the textbook, open-ended inquiry: "Mr. Williams, do you know why you are here today?"

"Kahn, uh huh, yeah...Kahn," I mumbled an uptight response.

"Who tried to con you?"

"Nobody. I'm Kahn, not Williams." I anxiously fidgeted with my hat. "Well... actually, I'm William, too."

"Oh, I see. And when was the first time you experienced this?"

From the note I saw her make, she suspected my boat was sinking due to schizophrenia. I realized my attempt to subtly correct her flip of my first and last name didn't work. Supposedly, she had misread my "chart" and, evidently, I had confused her even more. A minute into the encounter and I'd caused a leak in the scenario I was portraying

Now came my challenge to patch the hole. I necessarily had to alter her perception without unnecessarily creating anxiety over her error.

I leaned forward, gesturing toward her clipboard, and voiced an uneasy suspicion. "Is that what Don told you is wrong with me?"

Surely she had read on my "chart" that my son, Don, had brought me in for this evaluation. Hopefully, my reference to him, by name, would bail us out.

"Oh, I see…Don, you say." She hurriedly scribbled a third name into her notes as she benevolently continued. "Does Don visit you often?"

Oh, oh. The hole just got bigger. We were taking on water at an alarming rate. Not wanting to go out of character, I tried one last ploy to right the listing ship.

In my best impression of someone afflicted with paranoia, I twisted my hat even tighter and fretfully glanced into every corner of the room. Endeavoring to mix suspicion with fact, I responded. "Yes, David visits me often. He's my son. I don't see him in here, just like I don't actually see who is trying to steal from me. But, I know they are out there."

"Which one, Don, Con or William?"

And to think she thought it was my dinghy that was sinking.

QUESTION OF THE DAY:

Who actually cans the worms we're not supposed to open?

Normally, when I go to the pharmacy for a prescription, insurance covers most of the cost. Once, I did find a bone of contention in the can of worms my pharmacist opened.

20

Perplexing Prescription

This week, I needed to stop my Warfarin® pills and begin taking Lovenox® shots. The reason for this temporary switch of meds is not important. What is important is the cost involved. Or, I should say the battle that I became embroiled in—if not boiled over.

You see, my script for Warfarin costs me $12 for a three-month supply. When I went to pick up the Lovenox, the pharmacist advised me it would be $358 for the ten shots the doctor prescribed. I immediately inquired if the pharmacy had defib paddles...I was about to go into full cardiac arrest. THREE HUNDRED? Are the syringes gold?

Now, before I go any further, please understand that my comments were not an attack on the pharmacist. I visit her often and she is familiar with my frivolous humor. She is always extremely helpful, so my comments to her...and now reported here, were intended to be sarcastically humorous.

"No, Mr. Kaiser," she matter-of-factly stated. "It is a very expensive drug."

"How about a generic substitute for Lovenox?"

"This IS the generic, but it's still a hundred bucks a shot."

I advised her I was going to investigate my coverage at home and return. I checked the book. I'm not going to try to explain my Medicare Part D Formulary Book. It would probably be easier for me to explain Einstein's Theory of Relativity than the relatively theory-less formulary book. Bottom line: The generic of Lovenox at 150 ml is Tier 5 = blood curdling deductible and co-pay. Now, isn't that the height of irony? The thought of $350 co-pay curdling my blood when the drug itself is supposed to deter clotting.

Ah, but another inconceivable irony was that Lovenox per se is only Tier 3 and a lot less co-pay. Upon my return to the pharmacy, I showed her my formulary book and she checked my coverage. "I'm sorry, Mr. Kaiser. Lovenox doesn't come in 150 ml syringes. Only 300 ml vials."

"So, what do I do, drink it?"

"No, you stick the syringe in the vial and draw out the dosage."

"No problem. I remember drawing bacteria from a vial like that back in my college microbiology class. Gimme a few vials of that stuff and I'll be on my way."

After she regained some degree of composure, she offered, "Wait, let me see your formulary book. Maybe I can find a better alternative."

She put some info in the computer, checked my coverage and smiled broadly. "I can give you the generic drug in 80 ml syringes. You'll have to take two shots each night instead of one."

"No problem there. I'm sure Sue will be happy to stab me twice as much."

She called the doctor for his approval and filled the script. $12 for 16 shots at 80 ml each. Needless to say, I was delighted with the considerable reduction in cost for, effectively, the same medication and dosage as initially prescribed. Twelve bucks instead of $350? My blood was flowing freely again. I was thrilled.

Well, at first I was thrilled. But when the pharmacist explained the deal, I quickly went from the plus side of the emotional ledger to nonplussed. You see, the 80 ml dosage WAS FOR WOMEN. Men require larger dosages which cost more per shot. Soooo, what's the problem, you say. It makes sense, doesn't it? More drug, more money. Ah, but the syringes of double the dosage for men was not double the cost. Would you believe quadruple the co-pay? Oh no... no macho for me. I'll gladly get jabbed twice a day for the cost savings.

So, for a guy who often takes "shots" at women, I'm now going to take a woman's shot for about 10 days. Actually, it'll be two a day. But, hey...a man oughtta be tough enough for double the pokes.

QUESTION OF THE DAY:

If you don't give it your awl, would you be boring?

I have a great tendency to bore into everything with my awl...I mean, give my all in whatever I do. Sometimes, my all-in attitude becomes overaggressive and detrimental.

21

Post Op

When I asked the surgeon what she was actually going to do during arthroscopic surgery, she said, "Clean up".

Though I speculated that was a euphemism for her payday, it did not sound particularly troublesome for my knee. The original diagnosis was torn meniscus. Everyone I talked to who had experienced such an injury, spoke of fairly expedient recovery. Unfortunately, the surgeon found quite a bit more to "clean up." And I am most certainly not like most people.

In addition to cleaning up the torn cartilage, the surgeon felt it advisable to scrape the roughness from the back of my knee cap as well as smooth out some rough spots on a previously torn ACL. Combine that additional trauma for my knee with the effects of blood thinning Lovenox and Coumadin to ward off blood clots and it is not surprising that my knee bled internally more than for most folks.

And speaking of Lovenox, what irony in that brand name. First, they are shots—as in long needles thrust into my abdomen twice daily for a week.

Second, if I give myself the shots, it's a sure bet I'll bend the needle... after it's in my belly. Let's see... blood thinning agent... saber thrust... an autonomic reflex twitch of my hand and my abdomen would soon qualify as a camouflage hunting vest. So, considering my shots are administered by Sue, I suppose Love does have some connotation. But nox? Isn't nox a short form of noxious?

Yes, I'll admit blood thinners and extra scraping of my knee were contributors to slow healing, yet the deciding factor in my delayed recovery was my aggressive nature.

The doctor said crutches would be necessary for four or five days. Nevertheless, when I awoke after a considerable nap following surgery, it did not really hurt much to walk. And even the next morning, I felt no need for crutches. Oh, sure, some discomfort, but the macho-me ain't no wimp. Yeah, no pain, no gain.

I had a post-op appointment with the surgeon and then on to physical therapy. All without crutches. I was really feeling like I was going to beat the odds with a super quick recovery.

Then the residual, local anesthesia dissipated. MORPHINE! I WANT MORPHINE!!...and crutches.

QUESTION OF THE DAY:

Can a bald man part with his comb?

(22)

Relativity

While shaving, the mirror revealed an image far less than the fairest of all. Not only were my whiskers two days later than a five o'clock shadow, my sideburns needed a trim. Well, more to the point, if the hair lapping over my ears and my sparse topknot were bright red, I'd pass for Clarabell the Clown.

This image brought to my mind another application for the theory of relativity. In conjunction with my mirror appraisal of long sideburns and notable scarcity of hair at the top of my head, I mused about my follicly challenged pate. Though baldness is not overwhelmingly depressing for me, I did lament the days when I actually needed to carry a comb.

As a youth in the '60s, I needed both a comb and gobs of Suave to maintain the three-inch wave in my hair...and to keep the colic down, as well. Now, a frog jumping into our pond makes more of a wave than I can get to stand up with a whole tube of hair gel.

And, the colic that used to embarrass me? Well, it's still there, but you need a strong backlight to see it. Such a scenario did inspire raucous laughter from the grandkids. From the backseat of our van, they highlighted my static-lifted hair with blue light from a cell phone during a nighttime car ride. They are easily entertained.

Anyway, back to my mirrored image. I needed a side trim, so I went to see my stepdaughter, Kim, who's a hairdresser...on the side. From the following conversation, you may question which side.

"Say, Kim, my hair is in need of a trim." I was thinking cutters, but absentmindedly misspoke, "Do you have time to get out your curlers?"

Three other females within hearing distance joined Kim in a chorus of "Curlers, what do you need curlers for?"

Trying to cover my blunder, "Well, I...ah... I just wondered if curlers might give me a little more body on the top."

Chelsea chided, "How do you expect body from 3 hairs?"

Kim mumbled something about the fallacy of trying to work with something that's not there.

Amara, however, was much kinder and just covered her mouth and giggled.

So, you ask, other than the fact that they are relatives, what does all this have to do with the theory of relativity?

Well, when I got home, I happened by the mirror again. In contrast to the "before" mirror observation, there now seemed to be more hair on top. Ah, ha, I'm not nearly as bald as I thought. I just need to keep the hair on the sides very short. Then the hair on top will seem relatively long.

Nevertheless, as I pondered this theory in front of the mirror, I concluded there is also the law of diminishing returns applicable to the theory of relativity. A Mohawk would not be a viable option, no matter how short I have the sideburns trimmed.

QUESTION OF THE DAY:

When someone pulls your leg, why does it close your eyes to reality?

I confess. I am often guilty of pulling someone's leg. Sometimes it's an out-and-out April Fool's joke. Generally, though, I just try to facetiously twist reality.

Hospital PR

I have had many opportunities to interact with a wide variety of specialties involving hospital staff. For the most part, they have demonstrated sincerity while carrying out mundane tasks. Sometimes their sincerity muddles interactions with guys like me who try to interject levity into most every situation.

During one of my hospital stays, a young lady came into my room. She was not wearing scrubs or a white coat. Her businesslike attire suggested she was not there to draw blood. Although, I did wonder if her resistance to smile was to cover up fangs.

She introduced herself. I'll just use Janice to provide easy identity in this narrative, without clearly identifying her or the hospital. With perfunctory poise she explained she was there to fulfill a procedural responsibility.

Janice described her position with regard to Patient Relations. She concluded by asking, "How are you doing?" It amazes me how frequently that question was asked of me by people who have more access to my medical reports than I do.

"Doing?" I responded. "I'm doing just about nothing. Doctor's orders. Are you in a position to rectify that?"

Please understand that I did not speak those words with any animosity or disparaging inflections in my voice. I tried to ooze chocolate between each word. I, likewise, think there was some sugaring in her response. "No, I cannot change any of your restrictions. The doctors make those decisions without our input."

Incidentally, I actually think she wrote down that I was doing nothing. When she looked up from her clipboard, she inquired about the care I was getting from the nurses.

I took the opportunity to log a complaint. I shared an incident with Janice.

Earlier, I had pressed the call button. When the nurse arrived, I told her, "My phone is not functioning properly." She told me, "I didn't come in to answer the call button. I need to start a new Heparin bag."

I continued, but used a little more emphatic tone of voice to accentuate my story.

I think there is something wrong with the staff's priorities. I called for assistance in a matter of considerable importance to me and she excused herself from the challenging task of repairing my phone by attending to something so routine as changing an IV bag.

Janice was furiously writing on her clipboard, and somewhat remotely replied, "I have made a note of this, Mr. Kaiser."

At that moment, Ashley, the offending nurse came into the room. What great timing. I couldn't have written a better screenplay.

"There, Ashley, I told you you would regret ignoring my call for assistance. Now you're going to get it. I've logged a report that you won't fix my phone."

Ashley retorted matter-of-factly. "What's the big deal. You don't have any friends who'd call you anyway."

Janice's gasp would have maxed out a ventilation Spirometer. She became sufficiently pallid to warrant an IV of her own. It looked like all the starch came out of her suit as a noticeable slouch undermined her prim posture.

The PR gal's tension didn't last very long though. When she noticed the smiles on both Ashley's and my faces, color returned to hers.

I don't suppose that Janice actually turned in the report of my complaint, but I'm reasonably certain she did file a report. Without a doubt, she reported to the rest of the PR staff to be wary when entering my room.

QUESTION OF THE DAY:

A stitch in time saves nine what?

Stitches involve needles. I can't say that I have a phobia regarding needles, but my veins seem to have a strong aversion to them. My blood vessels seem to have an intrinsic avoidance system very adept at evading medicinal harpoons.

needled

Though I have not had extensive experience, there does seem to be one consistent thing about my stays in the hospital. Needles. Blood draws, injections and IVs are not only commonplace, I'm wondering if the nurses have a daily quota.

I would speculate that inserting an IV should score 5 points because nobody has to move them for 5 days. I suspect an injection with a short needle doesn't score quite as high as a hypodermic injection. Max points for use of a syringe which they withdraw from a scabbard.

Blood draws — which perversely occur an hour before you're awake enough to order breakfast — might not even be counted toward the nurse's quota. They are usually accomplished by an itinerant phlebotomist. They, themselves, might have quotas based on the number of vials drawn, rather than number of holes punched.

If a nurse's scoring is tallied by the number of holes they put in a patient, I am prime-time point potential. The nurses really rack up points trying to insert intravenous catheters into me. Apparently, my veins have a strong aversion to needles.

I don't flinch, but my veins are elusive. They squirm more than worms on a fishhook. When I was first admitted for my last hospital visit, no less than 3 nurses poked 4 holes without even the slightest hint of red.

Well, that's not exactly true. There was plenty of red bubbling up under the skin, but not in the vial. Each nurse would comment on how big a particular vein looked, but when the needle went in, the vein sidestepped as agilely as a matador does the bull's horns. By now, I've been categorically listed as hypodermically challenged.

Even with the frustration I caused them inserting the initial IV, it needed to be changed about day four. At the time the nurse wanted to tap a new hole, granddaughter Amara was visiting. Her mom suggested it was time to leave.

Amara wanted to watch. Now, Amara absolutely hates needles when they are aimed at her arm, but was eager to watch them poke me. I made a deal with her. If she promised not to throw a tantrum at her next blood draw, I would let her watch the nurse insert a new IV. Deal made. Amara got a double feature. The first poke predictably failed.

The second attempt was successful. With the new IV in place and operational, it was time for the nurse to remove the old IV. She advised those watching that there would likely be some "visible bleeding."

This time, Kim, Sue, and Papa, all told Amara, "It would be a good time for you to leave now."

"No, I want to stay," Amara compellingly interjected. "I wanna watch Papa bleed."

Oh, wow…my tears welled up over such an expression of love.

QUESTION OF THE DAY:

To what location do you take your shower?

Physical exertion, such as playing a softball game, generally produces tension, sweat and some aching muscles. All of this can be rinsed away and soothed by a hot shower. Sorry, but I simply soak in the spray — I don't actually take it anywhere.

25

No Ball This Year

Ah, yes…'tis Spring, …when a young man's fancy turns to love… and baseball. Okay, so maybe a 70-year-old man's fancy turns to softball. Before I was old enough to seriously contemplate romantic involvement with a girl, I romanced softball.

I truly enjoyed the game. Every Spring I'd get out my glove, smack the ball in the pocket a few times and head off for some hitting and fielding practice.

Not this year. The torn meniscus in my knee has not responded well to the surgery of last year. It's now in a brace most of the time. Granted, the last few years, I've run more like a hippo than a deer, but now, runnin' with a brace I'm slower than a slug pullin' an anvil.

However, running speed is not what's keeping me from playing. It is more a matter of reaction speed. From the first time I attempted to field a bouncing softball, my faulty reactions to bad hops has been painful. In my youthful years, the bruises to my body, as well as my confidence, healed quickly. Not so today.

Because I'm on a heavy dose of rat poison...aka Coumadin...a contusion from a not-so-soft ball could severely bruise more than my ego. I had to ask the doctor if he'd condone my playing softball. He inquired what position I played.

"I'm a pitcher," I told him.

"Whoa, that's much too close to the batter. The risk is too high for getting hit by a screaming liner. How about playing the outfield?"

"I run too long in one spot to play the outfield," I admitted.

Sue chimed in, "Besides, he'd fall down too much out there."

The doctor then asked if I could play first base. I agreed I could play that position.

"Good," he conceded, "that's far enough away from the plate."

"But Ed," Sue interjected, "you still have to run when you hit the ball. And you know how often you stumble getting out of the batter's box." Remind me not to take Sue to any more medical-softball consultations.

Yeah, I know. She's right. After all these years of playing the sport, it's automatic for my body to lean toward first base as it recoils from hitting the ball. The problem of late is my shoulders are squared up and headed for first about two steps before my shoes leave the batter's box.

Regrettably, a 6-foot, 4-inch frame with shoes two steps behind its hat, forms an obtuse angle ever increasing from its 90 degree start toward a 180 degree flat line...with the emphasis on flat. Inevitably my nose makes intimate contact with the base path. It is absolutely shameful to get up from such a sprawl with a chalk line from forehead to chin.

So, this year, in consideration of the doctor's advice and Sue's trepidation of my tripping, I'll probably be the ump behind the plate. Not much chance of injury there...unless the crowd starts throwing stuff at me.

QUESTION OF THE DAY:

Do two physicians make a paradox?

26

Difficult Patient

Although there are other stories in this book about me portraying a Standardized Patient, I was once involved in an MSU workshop where I only Simulated a patient. I had no standardized scenario to follow. I was simply to simulate a generic patient. This seminar was for doctors, not students.

The event was for licensed medical doctors coming to MSU for practical experiences in **Dealing with Difficult Patients**. No doubt, one or more of my personal physicians submitted my name as perfect for simulating such a patient.

The only briefing I received for this portrayal was a single paragraph describing me as having a serious heart problem, in the hospital, awaiting for the results of several tests.

I was specifically instructed to be impatient and ornery while the doctor was trying to find a way to deliver a rather scary prognosis. The exercise was to be accomplished by one physician, while the seminar leader and other participants observed.

The doctor began, "Hi, Mr. Smith, I'm doctor Brown. Would you mind if we chatted for a few minutes?"

"Chat…you want to chat? Last night my chest had two elephants dancing on it and this morning you want to chat?"

"I'm very sorry for your discomfort last evening. Are you comfortable this morning?"

"Are you serious? After the ER nurse's hasty shave, my chest has more wires than hair. I've got an IV jammed in my arm, an oxygen tube stuffed up my nose and another tube filling a zip-lock baggie down there."

I could hear a few snickers from the observers, but he fought back a grin and kindly responded. "It's going to be a little while before all the test results are back. I'd like to discuss a few things with you while we wait."

Accepting his holistic approach I replied, "I guess I don't have much choice. Go ahead with your questions."

He proceeded to inquire about several incidental aspects of my life and then got around to my faith. I admitted that my wife drags me to church, but that I do believe in God.

"And do you believe in prayer?" he inquired.

"I s'pose so. But I believe in doctors a whole lot more than prayer."

"Do you think doctors can be an answer to prayer?"

"How's that?"

"Well, I'm sure you've seen 'faith healers' on TV bringing about 'miracles'."

"Let me tell ya, Doc," I scowled, "You put your hand on my forehead and I'm outa here. How's that for a miracle healing!"

Even a quick hand over his eyes as he looked down at my chart could not conceal his chuckle. And when he did look up, he could not hold back a snorted giggle.

I think we both failed. He was not able to stay in control and I flopped at being ornery. But maybe we both had a good day.

QUESTION OF THE DAY:

Why is it acceptable to put your finger in your ear, but not in your nose?

Wearing hearing aids creates an ear canal environment close to that of a terrarium. What's worse is that everything that attempts to grow there, itches. I'm very glad it is socially acceptable to itch what tickles there. I cannot be without my hearing aids, yet sometimes I may reject available options.

27

Hearing Aid Options

Earlier this week I visited a VA clinic. No, not a clinic in the state of VA, but one in a Veterans Administration building. So, you ask, have I given up on my private-sector physician?

Not at all. I went to the VA because of private-sector sticker shock... as in, "Let's stick'r in his ear, and shock the hard-of-hearing guy." I have utilized hearing aids for many years now. Over time the aids have advanced from volume enhancements to computers which can produce pitches my ears can hear from sounds my ears cannot discern. That's the good news. Bad news is that such 'state of the art' is priced higher than pen and ink art by Van Gogh.

Medicare won't pay for hearing aids. Getting a Miracle Ear would cost me an arm and a leg. There's definitely something wrong with the logic of such a trade.

I've investigated some *low cost* hearing aids that claim to "never miss a sound." I cannot figure out how they can say that. It's physiologically impossible for me to hear some sounds. The only logic to such a claim is that the aid doesn't *miss* the sound even if it can't pass it onto my ear drum. Logical, yet irrationally absurd. Despite their claim, I cannot detect high frequency sounds.

Sue accuses me of selective hearing at a high frequency. Not the high-frequency of sound waves. Rather, my high frequency of denying I can hear her restrictive pronouncements. She contends that I tune out things I don't want to hear. I wonder how long it will be before technology devises the algorithm for such intuitive tuning.

Television ads often infer super sensitive listening devices. I saw one which depicted a hearing aid capable of snooping in on gossip from across the room. I think it immediately preceded ads for Aphrodisiac Aftershave, bottled Diet Water, Look-young Liniment and X-Ray glasses. I nodded off during the X-Ray ad so I'm not sure how they manage to look through a wall but not the people on the other side. But then I never quite understood that about the super dude with a red "S" on his chest, either.

Speaking of superpowers, I do have the option to purchase a **Rechargeable Bionic Aid.** I'm not exactly sure whether it's Steve Austin's or Jaime Sommers' cloned ear. However, I shouldn't worry about that. No doubt it's masculine looking. After all, it is Lee Major's company which markets the **Bionic Aid.** Hey, I don't make this stuff up. I just report what I see, without any concern for credibility.

I do have a concern with regard to "rechargeable" hearing aids, though. I'm not sure I'm ready for a solar panel implanted on top of my head. But, I suppose that would lessen the chances of sun burn on my scalp.

By the way, scalp has a double meaning in purchase of the "Bionic Aid." The prominent, large, enhanced font, numbers on the ad are $14.95...plus S&H which nobody advertises in large font. Also in the small, faded, infinitesimal print at the bottom of the screen: *This introductory offer is followed by 3 easy payments of...* I'm not sure what the dollar figure was as it disappeared from the screen too quickly. Okay, so bionic is not realistic either.

Concluding that *inexpensive* is directly proportional to *credibility*, and with my financial liquidity being atomized with liquid nitrogen, I'm hoping the VA will provide new hearing aids for me. That way I won't have to pay through the nose to hear with my ears.

QUESTION OF THE DAY:

If a tomato is a fruit, why isn't it ever in a fruit salad?

Some questions of the day have potentially rational answers. Botanically, a tomato is a fruit; yet culinary folks categorically consider it a vegetable. I suppose taste trumps technicality, so this is one fruit of a vine never to be in a fruit cocktail.

$\left(28\right)$

Do Eye Care

In a discussion of eye care, a friend recommended tomatoes as being beneficial to maintaining good eyesight. My mom, on the other hand, consistently encouraged me to eat carrots so I would not need glasses. That prophecy did not come to fruition as I still eat lots of carrots AND wear glasses. But Mom didn't promote tomatoes. Because I do care about my eye care, I decided to investigate what food products may have a positive influence on vision. In this age of the Internet, I could forego a trip to the library.

Admittedly, I did not read any of the googled articles in depth. Who, besides a doctoral student, has time, or inclination, to read technical articles in depth? I searched for key words, perused nearby commentary from which I easily wandered into my own conclusions.

The first thing I discovered was that tomatoes are not at the top of the list of eye-degeneration remedies. That hierarchy is headed by Kale.

I'm not sure, but I think he drove a race car...Yarborough might have been his last name.

No, I'm confusing Yarborough with Marlboro and cigarette smoke is definitely not good for the eyes.

As I mentioned, I didn't read much further than the searched word "kale" but I'm sure the article alluded to the fact that race drivers have excellent eyesight capable of focusing through clouds of engine smoke and flying debris. Whatever Kale says, follow his advice. Oh, oh! It wasn't my eyes failing me. The phonetics of kale and Cale really got me off track.

Back on track, I searched for second item on the list of good advice for eyecare—eat spinach. Well, now, that's a no brainer. Hellooooo, PopEYE and spinach. Who needs to read any further?

Then the article listed a couple veggies which are distant cousins of blueberries—which are already in my dietary prohibition. The article specifically stated…and I quote, "peas and brussel sprouts provide clearer vision." Well, there you have it, ladies and gentlemen. The credibility of any advice following the misspelling of Brussels sprouts went downhill faster than those balls of green mush can roll.

Even though lima beans don't roll as well as peas, I didn't even look to see if they were on the list of eye-care goodies. My eyes tear up just thinking about lima beans and I can't even say "succotash" without gagging.

I abandoned that particular article and renewed my search for tomato benefits. My search found a far more authoritative source with a rather astounding revelation: "Tomatoes have antioxidants in them which reduce the amount of free radicals in our body."

Whoa…what do I need antioxidants for. Is my body rusting from the inside out? I really must reduce my iron intake…and soon.

And what's with the radicals? In my body? I have no specific political affiliation. I'm non-partisan. Of course, I must admit that radicals often do get under my skin. But they don't stay free for long. My lymphatic system, kidneys, and bowels each trap and extradite radicals.

The article further advised me that free radicals are known to have degenerative effects. EXACTLY! Who didn't already know that? It's those miserable radicals that emit the aroma accompanying that which is discharged by my kidneys and bowels.

Though most of the Internet articles keyed on fruits and vegetables as good for eye care, I believe that the best eyesight in nature belongs to meat eaters. Bring on the steak…forget the veggies.

QUESTION OF THE DAY:

Have you ever been tempted to put "Doctor" on a form that asks, "In case of emergency, contact:"?

It seems that the concept of electronically connecting all "health providers" is lost in cyberspace. Invariably, I still have to complete several pages of questions at every new medical office I visit. Oh, and sometimes I remotely fill in the blanks over the phone.

29

Gerber Insurance

We decided to switch our Medigap insurance carrier. I think it's a game the insurance companies play. They entice you to switch to their company with deeply discounted rates, then routinely raise their rates each year and hope you stay with them. Well, we found that Gerber no longer professes, "...Babies are our only business." They now insure as many old folks as infants and, right now, their Medigap rates are considerably lower than our current carrier.

The irony is that Gerber is a subsidiary of Mutual of Omaha...our current carrier. Hey, for a hundred bucks a month savings, I'll play their game. Despite the fact of "guaranteed continuous coverage," they still needed to investigate our current health. Well, at least *my* current health. When we applied, they accepted Sue's fill-in-the-blanks assessment, carte blanche. Mine must have had a flat tire on the cart. They needed to speak with me for clarification.

I cannot explain what happens to me in the midst of most phone conversations. I suspect there is a virus in my handset which inevitably worms its way through my ears and into my psyche.

After the Gerber representative completed a cursory validation of my personal information and a few generalized questions in regard to my health, she inquired about my prescriptions drugs.

She proceeded. "Do you take any prescription medications?"

I advised her that I would read her my meds from a printed list. I don't trust my memory for this specific inquiry. I change drugs more often than I change the oil in the car. Additionally, drugs with names of 8 or more syllables, severely diminish my accuracy. Even 3-syllable generic names don't have much sensibility to them. I mean, what's the sense of Omeprozole. Why not call it "NoBurp" or "UnGERD". I could remember that.

After I had reported my entire list of medications and dosages, she asked, "Are you still taking the Hydrocondriactomenosomething?"

"Ahhh," I hesitated, "I don't recognize that drug."

"My records indicate it was prescribed by Doctor Ben deVious. Is he your personal physician?"

"Ah... yes... doctor devious...sounds familiar. But I don't see hydro-anything on my drug list."

"He scripted it last October. It is a very potent, narcotic, analgesic."

"Oh, yeah…now I remember. Ooooh, that's good stuff. I gotta get some more of that."

Anyway, on with the interrogation she inquired, "Do you smoke?"

"No."

"Do you drink?"

"Mostly water."

"I assure you, we are not concerned with your intake of water," she kindly clarified.

"Okay, so maybe I do indulge in ice tea or a Coke now and then…. nothing to an excess, though."

I could sense she was repressing a chuckle. The challenge was begging for fulfillment. After finally getting a "no alcohol" from me, she moved on the next topic.

"Are you able to do your own work around the house or do you hire it out?"

"Oh, I do most of it, yes. My wife often gives me a list. I'm very capable of menial tasks."

This time she released a muffled, yet encouraging, chuckle before continuing, "Are you confined?"

"Confined?"

"Yes. That is, unable to get out in public?"

"Well, Sue doesn't allow me to be in public without her supervision. But we do go out often. Oh, and I returned my electronic tether to the sheriff last week, so I can go just about anywhere I want now."

That did it. She was no longer able to repress her laughter.

I'm not certain whether she had reached the end of her list of questions, or she no longer saw a need to continue. She thanked me for my time and said I'd be hearing from Gerber very soon.

Apparently, that phone encounter did not adversely affect my insurability. We soon received notification that my coverage had been approved and that a detailed policy statement would be forthcoming in the mail. When it arrives, I'll have to peruse it closely to see if there are any mental illness disclaimers in force.

QUESTION OF THE DAY:

If you bit into a byte, how many bits would RAM into your mouth?

In computer lingo, a byte is composed of 8 bits. It baffles me, why the coiner of the term byte, didn't also decide "byt" would be the logical subdivision of a byte. "Bit" was already muddled with a dozen definitions not counting a myriad of idioms. For those not particularly computer literate, though RAM is the acronym for Random Access Memory, in small case letters it could be the verb denoting the method of getting bits into a byte.

30

Painful Byte

Yesterday I went to the doctor. Nothing serious. It was just a follow-up visit for a malady which is improving. When Sue and I arrived, the waiting room had a couple people ahead of me. This was not discouraging. It's a small town practice with two doctors and they are rarely "behind" by more than a few minutes. Besides, we were early for my appointment.

As expected, one of the two waiting patients was called in from the waiting room to an examination room. The second patient was beckoned from the waiting room a short while later. I know it was a very short time as Sue only had time to show me cute cupcakes and a Fruity Pebbles caterpillar in a magazine. We don't get subscriptions to magazines. We just go to the doctor once a month.

Anyway, with the waiting room empty, the doctors seemed back on schedule. My appointment time arrived. A couple of other patients arrived. The beckoning nurse did not.

Nor did she make an appearance before my daily pill of *groggy* got into my blood stream. Because I'd not yet gone into full snore mode, my nap was likely quite short, yet when I opened my eyes, almost all the chairs in the waiting room were taken. Highly unusual. Fortunately, there was one left for the doctor to sit in when he came into the waiting room.

Now, despite the small town nature of this office, my personal physician does not normally come and sit in the waiting room. However, when he did exactly that, his facial expression demonstrated enough distress that I thought maybe he was getting in line to see the other doctor.

He slumped into the chair and dejectedly greeted us, "Hi, how are you this afternoon?"

Well, don't that beat all. I was there for his assessment of me. If my answer to his opening question would have been, "Just fine", I wouldn't have been there to see him.

Yeah, I realize such a question is a generic *ice breaker*, not a meaningful inquiry. He continued to explain why he had come out to see us in the waiting room, "the computes are down. I've tried to reboot them, but get nothing. I can't even get your names to come up on the screen."

I tried to help with that aspect, "Hi, Doctor, I'm Ed."

This was not a startling revelation to him as the rest of the room was full of females. Also, considering that I see him every couple weeks, my attempt at humor wasn't startling to him, either. I think it did relieve some of his tension though, and brought a smile to some of the dour faces in the room. However, no amount of levity can lighten the burdensome vulnerability of this electronic age. Some of the bytes in his system had become infected.

The doctor went on, "Without the computer, I'm dead in the water." He's a great physician, but not so good with word choices. It wasn't even metaphorically accurate as the receptionist assured me she had not spilled coffee-maker water on the keyboard.

I am not intending this to have disparaging inferences about my doctor's practice, but we certainly have become as vulnerable to electronic maladies as physical afflictions.

To order additional copies of this book
and to see other books published by Buttonwood Press
visit us online at www.buttonwoodpress.com.

Buttonwood Press offers wholesome, entertaining, if not
captivating, reading for all ages — Fictional murders
in various Michigan locations, National Park Mysteries
for children ages 7-11, a pre-teenage Fantasy series as
well as more of Ed Kaiser's humor.

Also, visit my blog at www.fridayfrivolities.com.